SERIOUS GAMES IN EDUCATION

SERIOUS GAMES IN EDUCATION

– A Global Perspective

Edited by
Simon Egenfeldt-Nielsen,
Bente Meyer & Birgitte Holm Sørensen

AARHUS UNIVERSITY PRESS |

Serious Games in Education – a Global Perspective
© The authors and Aarhus University Press 2011
Cover design: Camilla Jørgensen, Trefold
Design: Narayana Press
Printed by: Narayana Press, Gylling

ISBN 978 87 7934 705 2

AARHUS UNIVERSITY PRESS

Aarhus
Langelandsgade 177
8200 Århus N

Copenhagen
Tuborgvej 164
2400 København NV

www.unipress.dk

INTERNATIONAL DISTRIBUTORS:

Gazelle Book Services Ltd.
White Cross Mills
Hightown, Lancaster, LA1 4XS
United Kingdom
www.gazellebookservices.co.uk

The David Brown Book Company
Box 511
Oakville, CT 06779
USA
www.oxbowbooks.com

CONTENTS

PREFACE   7

1. STATE OF THE ART

GAME-BASED LEARNING: A REVIEW OF THE STATE OF THE ART   21
Patrick Felicia
Simon Egenfeld-Nielsen

2. METHODS

2 A. DESIGN-BASED ACTION RESEARCH   47
Rikke Magnussen & Birgitte Holm Sørensen

2 B. MAKING CONNECTIONS – GLOBAL AND LOCAL ISSUES IN
RESEARCHING THE POLICY OF SERIOUS GAMES IN EDUCATION   59
Bente Meyer, Birgitte Holm Sørensen, Thorkild Hanghøj, & Lars Birch Andreasen

2 C. MULTI-SITED ANALYSIS OF GAME-BASED LEARNING   84
Bente Meyer

3. EDUCATIONAL DESIGN

EDUCATIONAL DESIGN FOR SERIOUS GAMES   101
Birgitte Holm Sørensen

4. TEACHERS AND SERIOUS GAMES

4 A. TEACHER ROLES AND POSITIONINGS IN
RELATION TO EDUCATIONAL GAMES   125
Thorkild Hanghøj & Christian Engel Brund

4 B. EDUCATIONAL DESIGN FOR LEARNING GAMES
WITH A FOCUS ON THE TEACHER'S ROLES   137
Birgitte Holm Sørensen & Bente Meyer

5. GAME AND PLAY

5 A. LEARNING GAMES AND THE DISRUPTIVE EFFECTS OF PLAY   153
Carsten Jessen

5 B. A GAME MAGICALLY CIRCLING   170
Stine Ejsing-Duun

6. GAME-BASED LEARNING'S STRUGGLE FOR ADAPTATION

INTERNATIONAL SURVEY ON THE EXPERIENCES
AND PERCEPTIONS OF TEACHERS   187
Simon Egenfeldt-Nielsen

PREFACE

INTRODUCTION

This book attempts to address the current need for more theoretically and empirically founded knowledge about game-based learning in a global context.

Gaming is growing significantly in importance. It used to be mostly about entertainment; now it is about almost everything else.. Serious games have benefited from this omnipresence, but they have also helped drive the transition by showing that games can be so much more than the mindless computer games played by teenage boys. Over the last twenty years the value of the games industry has increased from 15 billion to 75 billion EU, and each week the population spend around three billion hours playing (McGonigal 2011). People play in a variety of different ways: on their phones, on their televisions, on Facebook, or elsewhere on the internet. The number of platforms, channels, and genres offered to all sorts of audiences is immense, and the games industry seems to have cracked the code for making gaming a mainstream activity.

Just ten years ago, games were perceived in a very different way. Ask somebody to think of a game, and ten years ago they would probably have said *Counter Strike*; today there is a much broader variety of games to choose from, though many people would probably say *Angry Birds*, which is a much more mainstream game experience. Throughout this expansion, serious games have played a large role and it seems unavoidable that they will continue to have a larger and larger impact on the game market. This is especially true with regard to the barriers preventing greater penetration in areas such as education and healthcare, and in the corporations. As these slowly succumb the market will grow even more rapidly. Market research companies support this; IDATE, for example, predicts a growth from 1.5 billion in 2010 to 10.2 billion EU in 2015 (IDATE 2010).

Even though the dramatic increase in the market has only happened recently, the idea of using game-based learning is hardly new. Throughout the last forty years at least it is possible to trace a continuous interest in the area, though its strength varies (Abt 1970, Loftus & Loftus 1983, Egenfeldt-Nielsen 2007). Looking over the landscape today, things look promising with many active research projects, conferences, and initiatives, as well as media coverage. However, one key challenge remains: the lack of game-based learning as an integrated part of formal education. Game-based learning continues to be an exotic spice for many educators.

It would hardly be the first time that a technology he failed to deliver on its promises, turning out to nothing more than a fad (Cuban 2001). However, the continuous interest in game-based learning (Ito 2008, Egenfeldt-Nielsen 2007) and mounting evidence for its efficiency (Sitzmann & Elly 2010) suggest that there is a real potential. Many research overviews within the broad area of learning from video games have appeared in the past twenty years (i.e. Cavallari et al. 1992, Dempsey et al. 1996, McGrenere 1996). These serve as a viable starting point in combination with overviews that are more recent, inclusive, and thorough (i.e. de Freitas 2007, Kirriemuir & McFarlane 2003, Mitchell & Savill-Smith 2004, Squire 2002). In addition to the literature on learning from video games, there are a number of useful overviews of learning from simulations (Bredemeier & Greenblat 1981, Clegg 1991, Dorn 1989, Leemkuil et al. 2000, Randel et al. 1992, Van Sickle 1986, Wentworth & Lewis 1973). Most of these studies identify weaknesses in the use of the technology, but generally have positive conclusions to make about game-based learning, when games are used in effective ways.

When we look back over this previous research, it becomes clear that two areas have largely been overlooked. First of all, the critical role of the educator as a facilitator, gatekeeper, and enabler of serious games is often downplayed. Secondly, the comparisons across regions are limited, which limits the potential to transfer best practice, research results, and developed games across borders. This hinders the availability, adaptation, and quality of serious games, ultimately holding back the maturation of the market.

In this book we draw on research from a project on *Serious Games on a Global Market Place*, which was carried out during a four-year period from 2007-2011. The *Serious Games* project has been innovative in the field of game-based learning in a number of ways. Firstly, the project looked at educational gaming from a global perspective, comparing classroom practices, educational policy, and curricula in countries across Europe and Asia. Though it had a primarily Nordic perspective on game-based learning, and drew on Nordic traditions for play and learning, the aim of the project has been to understand how serious games are perceived and used in education worldwide and how they can be developed for a global educational market. This has, for instance, entailed following specific games into classrooms and homes with the purpose of studying national variations in educational traditions, curricula, and assessments, as well as marketing and distribution.

Secondly, with regard to the concept of the market, the project has ad-

dressed the issue of how serious games can be developed in collaboration between researchers, industrial game developers, and users. This has
involved issues of educational design and marketing, and challenges in
research industry collaboration brought about by new connections between
public and private actors and between nation states and global actors in
education. Throughout the project, research has relied on the products and
experiences of companies and game developers to develop knowledge about
the challenges, design, and assessment of serious games. Two serious game
concepts were studied: Mingoville, a game-based platform for teaching and
learning English targeted at young learners (age 9-12) (www.mingoville.
com), and Global Conflicts, a serious game aimed at teaching and learning
history, geography, and citizenship education in secondary schools (www.
globalconflicts.eu). Both of these educational games have been understood
as open game designs to be developed and studied in and through practice
in collaboration with the companies.

A NOTE ON TERMINOLOGY

Over the years the idea of using games for learning has been termed differently. The most frequent terms are 'game-based learning', 'serious games', and
'edutainment'. Although there are no tight definitions of any of these terms,
they each reflect different aspects of the concept'. 'Edutainment' and 'serious
games' are the oldest terms, whereas game-based learning' is increasingly
being used to refer to the use of games in schools. 'Serious games' was first
coined by Clark Abt in his book *Serious Games* from 1970.

> *Reduced to its formal essence, a game is an activity among two or more independent*
> *decision-makers seeking to achieve their objectives in some limiting context. A more*
> *conventional definition would say that a game is a context with rules among adver-*
> *saries trying to win objectives. We are concerned with serious games in the sense*
> *that these games have an explicit and carefully thought-out educational purpose*
> *and are not intended to be played primarily for amusement. C. Abt (1970, p. 6).*

Abt focused exclusively on non-electronic games but the term caught on
in 2002 when Woodrow Wilson started the Serious Games initiative, led
initially by Ben Sawyer. Serious games had relevance in all areas including
health, military, school, museums, etc. This was in contrast to 'edutainment',
which was labelled in the 1980s, and which referred primarily to children's
products that combined learning and games. Edutainment had a product

focus that became increasingly problematic in research circles and slowly the term 'game-based learning' took over. 'Game-based learning' is primarily used for games and learning targeted at the educational system, and emphasises the importance of the context of use rather than the product per se.

Throughout the book we use the concept of serious games to describe the phenomena that we are researching and developing. It is used primarily as a generic term to refer to a second generation of educational games, defined as digital games and equipment with an agenda beyond entertainment. In this sense we are using the serious games concept to break free of the somewhat dated and limited edutainment formula, even though we acknowledge that edutainment is still a very successful and extremely significant actor on the global education market – especially in preschool learning (Scanlon & Buckingham 2004). In the book we also use affiliated terms such as 'learning games', 'game-based learning' and 'educational games/gaming'. These terms are accepted in and used by the academic community as well as by game developers, and point to the fact that what characterises games is not only their 'seriousness' – as opposed to their affiliations with the 'fun' of edutainment – but the variety of roles and functions they can have in teaching and learning. In addition to this the concepts of game-based learning, educational games, and learning games may, as argued above, underline the processes of learning involved in doing gaming, rather than the inherent qualities in the game 'itself', which is an important distinction, we feel, in the discussion and exploration of what games 'are' and (can) 'do'.

THE CHAPTERS OF THE BOOK

The aims of this book and the associated project have, as described above, been manifold. We have sought to understand the impact, distribution, design, and use of serious games through both empirical and theoretical knowledge. We have worked towards establishing theoretical models that are able to predict the potential of serious games globally, and attempted to generate theoretical concepts and practical methods for innovative product development on the basis of these models. Finally, we have aimed at understanding practical barriers to the use of serious games, variations in student game competencies, and approaches to integrating games into teaching practices. These different perspectives are reflected in the structure of the book which deals with methodological issues, policy of games and ICT, classroom studies, and theoretical approaches to the design of serious games. The contents of the individual chapters will be described below for the benefit of the reader.

CHAPTER ONE

Any study of game-based learning must situate itself in the field of research to which it is contributing. In chapter one Patrick Felicia and Simon Egenfeldt-Nielsen give a thorough outline of the field of game-based learning (GBL) through a review of state of the art technologies. In the review, Felicia and Egenfeldt-Nielsen account for and discuss, on the basis of current research, a number of central issues in the field of game-based learning. For instance, how is GBL employed? What characterises digital games for learning? Which tools are employed to design and develop GBL? Other aspects of GBL discussed are its educational features and the question of why one should consider GBL compared to other traditional teaching methods; finally the paper accounts for different aspects of the empirical evidence that supports the use of GBL. The paper ends by looking into the future of GBL and proposes some research topics for the game ahead.

CHAPTER TWO

The focus of chapter two is mainly methodological, i.e. it takes up the question of how we can research games in classrooms as well as in informal learning contexts in global settings. It may be argued that one of the main characteristics of game-based teaching and learning is that it only plays a brief and often provisional role in the everyday world of schooling. Thus, it is almost by definition difficult to locate and study the (possibly) emergent practices of teaching and learning through games. As a consequence of the marginal role of serious games in curricula and classrooms, experimental set-ups may be needed in classrooms or with teachers that will enable researchers to study the phenomenon of game-based learning and teaching. Therefore different kinds of interventions are inherent in the study of game-based learning, even though there may be significant differences between forms of interventions – for instance, conducting ethnographically inspired studies that require researchers to engage with the everyday practices of teachers and students as opposed to more experimental studies that rely on exploratory set-ups. Taken in its general sense, it can be argued that it is impossible to conduct an empirical study on the actual use of learning games without some form of intervention.

Another aspect of researching serious games involves locating the use and distribution of game-based learning in the global market. How are games used in classrooms and homes in different geographical and national locations? How does policy intervene in or define the role of game-based learning? How do these uses and policies become accessible to research and how can they be compared? These are some of the questions raised by the papers in this chapter.

In their paper "Design-based action research", Rikke Magnussen and Birgitte Holm Sørensen review the methodological approaches of design-based research and action research and discuss some of the implications of applying these methods to game research. Both methods, the authors argue, involve combining empirical educational research with the theory-driven design of learning environments. However, whereas action research aims at changing attitudes or behaviour by involving participants in the different phases of designing environments for change, design-based research has a strong focus on theory-based design and implementation of technologies and artefacts as part of the learning environment. In the paper, the empirical focus is on the integration of the game Global Conflict: Latin America in a local school practice with the involvement of game developers, researchers, students, and teachers in the different phases of the game-based educational scenario. With the aim of developing approaches to modulate and integrate new game designs into school education, Magnussen and Sørensen suggest a design-based research approach inspired by action research with a focus on inviting teachers and players into the various phases of development of designs, intervention, redesigns, and analysis of design interventions.

In "Making connections – global and local issues in researching the policy of serious games in education", Bente Meyer, Birgitte Holm Sørensen, Thorkild Hanghøj, and Lars Birch Andreasen explore the effects of policy on game-based learning in four country studies, on Denmark, Portugal, Vietnam, and the UK. The study looks at how serious games are integrated into formal education as an aspect of digital literacy initiatives in policy, i.e. as connected to state endorsed strategies for the implementation of ICTs in schools. This requires an understanding of the role of game-based learning in connection with the economic growth and development of nation states as well as global tendencies in educational policy, for instance the 'marketization' of schooling, standardisation of testing and curricula, decentralisation of management and school choice, and the deskilling of teachers. The four case studies chosen for this paper represent different cultural and geographical positions in the world as well as diverging and converging approaches to the dissemination of ICT in education and generally point to the marginal position of serious games in educational policies, with significant exceptions.

SERIOUS GAMES IN EDUCATION

Finally, in her paper "Comparative studies in game-based language learning: a discussion of methodology", Bente Meyer focuses on the issue of studying game-based learning in global contexts through ethnographical methods. The paper discusses how global uses of serious games can be followed by research, where the intention is to understand how different cultural contexts for the use of game-based learning can be compared. Comparative methodologies can, Meyer argues, be difficult frameworks for understanding how and where game-based learning takes place, as the basis for comparison is often national frameworks for teaching and learning, and as learning games, actors, and contexts are not stable. Therefore, she proposes that approaching the study of game-based learning through multi-sited ethnography can contribute to the understanding of how serious games become part of teaching and learning. The empirical focus of the paper is an analysis of fieldwork done with the game-based platform Mingoville, which is a new type of learning material that cannot be fully understood and studied within the borders of a national education culture.

CHAPTER THREE

Chapter three focuses on the construction of a concept for educational design of serious games. Such a concept is needed at two levels of game-based learning: first in the construction of the game itself where a number of questions are raised which need to be taken into account in connection with the game design; and secondly in the usage of the game in lessons within various subject-specific and cross-curricular contexts where issues of educational design become relevant regarding, for example, planning, and teacher and pupil participation.

On the basis of the project Serious Games on a Global Market Place, Birgitte Holm Sørensen in the paper "Educational design for serious games" proposes a concept for an educational design incorporating theories of didactics and of learning including formal and informal learning, games, play, communication and multimodality, and various pedagogical approaches. This concept furthermore includes reflection on children and children positioned as pupils, as well as the role of the teacher in relation to serious games. The theoretical foundation for this educational design has its roots within constructivist, experience-oriented, and social learning theories including formal and informal learning, didactic categories such as teacher and pupil positions, relations and roles, forms of learning, and theories about games, play, communication, and multimodality.

CHAPTER FOUR

Teachers are central, we propose, to the process of integrating and developing the use of serious games in the classroom. In this chapter it is argued that educational game research has generally tended to neglect the crucial role of the teacher in choosing, preparing for, teaching, and evaluating the use of serious games. The chapter examines two aspects of teacher engagement in serious games, based on the empirical findings of the serious games project: first of all the paper by Thorkild Hanghøj and Christian Engel Brund focuses on the roles available to teachers when using serious games in the classroom and the ways in which teachers take up these roles. Secondly, the paper by Bente Meyer and Birgitte Holm Sørensen discusses and gives examples of the ways in which games can be designed to include and engage teachers.

Focusing on "Teacher Roles and Positionings in Relation to Educational Games", Thorkild Hanghøj and Christian Engel Brund argue that in order to understand how teachers facilitate educational games, it is necessary both to consider how different game modalities enable different teacher roles and also how teachers position themselves in relation to games. Hanghøj and Brund begin their paper by presenting a theoretically and empirically based framework for understanding how teachers facilitate games by shifting through the roles of instructor, playmaker, guide, and explorer. Next, they analyse and discuss whether the model can be extended to describe a group of 19 secondary teachers' approaches to the educational computer game series Global Conflicts (GC). The empirical analysis is based on positioning theory and multimodal theory and falls into two parts. In the first part, the authors analyse how the teachers enacted the GC games in different classroom settings. Next, they analyse a series of pre-game interviews with teachers and discuss how the teachers positioned themselves in relation to the GC games – both in relation to their general pedagogical beliefs and in relation to more specific assumptions about how to teach with the GC games.

The approach of Sørensen and Meyer to the problem of teacher involvement in game-based learning focuses on the issue of serious game design. Game activity, it may be argued, has often been conceptualised as student-centred, which may be why serious game designs have neglected to include the teacher. Therefore, the paper "Educational Design for Learning Games with a focus on the teacher's roles" deals with the challenges related to the development of an educational design for learning games that specifically address teachers. The focus is on how instructional and introductory texts that are integrated into specific game-based platforms support teachers' involvement in game-based learning, and how and why these texts can be developed as part of the educational design of game-based learning. In the paper Meyer and Sørensen conceptualise introductory texts for teachers as paratexts, following Genette's terminology. Based on empirical studies the paper analyses different ways of employing paratexts directed to the teachers and in the educational design of game-based learning environments, and discuss what design aspects should be considered when addressing the teachers.

CHAPTER FIVE

The project Serious Games on a Global Market Place studied the role of serious games in formal education and informal learning as well as the role of play in relation to games and learning. The role of play in learning has traditionally held an important position in Nordic studies of children and children's cultures and one aspect of the Serious Games on a Global Market Place project has therefore been to develop games that can stimulate children and young people to engage in physical play and learning. This chapter presents some of the theoretical and empirical perspectives involved in linking the study of game-based learning to the activities of play and playful experiences.

In "Learning Games and the Disruptive Effects of Play", Carsten Jessen discusses aspects of the relationship of play to games and learning based on a discussion of, among others, Sutton-Smith's seminal work *The Ambiguity of Play* (1997). In his paper Jessen argues that most current scholars seem to agree that video games are an untapped resource in the field of education and that the main problems are bad game design and teachers lacking knowledge about games. However, neither games nor teachers nor the combination thereof seems to constitute the whole problem, Jessen proposes. Instead, the phenomenon *play* disrupts the interplay between games and learning, which, in a pedagogical context, is expected to be a productive combination. The point is, Jessen concludes, that acknowledging games and play as independent cultural phenomena enables one to view the learning processes more clearly. Instead of becoming hypnotised by the motivational power of gaming, it becomes possible to analyse players' ways of learning as well as the question of whether the players have a well-functioning *learning community* and an accessible *learning network* consisting of more experienced players.

Finally, in "A game magically circling", Stine Ejsing-Duun analyses the relationship between players, the game world, and the ordinary world in connection with alternative reality games and location based games (ARGs and LBGs). These games use technology to create play and a game world in everyday scenarios. Many game researchers refer to the idea of the 'magic circle', initially introduced by Johan Huizinga (1993), when analysing a game situation. Ejsing-Duun argues that when a game is placed in the everyday scene it is not possible to uphold the idea of a magic circle. The point is that we need another understanding of the limits between the ordinary world and the game world when playing alternative reality games. To develop this understanding the chapter draws on Michael Apter's theory about motivation and play, where the focus is on the players' approach to the game instead of on strict rules that ensure the magic circle, as suggested by Huizinga (1993) and Salen and Zimmerman (2004). Apter's view makes it possible to integrate the ordinary world and the game world without losing the magic of the game. Ejsing-Duun proposes that in terms of alternative reality games it makes sense to talk about integration of the everyday space into the game rather than the game's separation from the ordinary world.

CHAPTER SIX

In the last chapter of the book, "Game-based learning struggling for adaptation – international survey on the experience and perception among teachers", Simon Egenfeldt-Nielsen presents the results from an online survey undertaken in Denmark, Finland, Norway, Portugal, and the United States with 275 respondents. The survey aimed to provide an understanding of teachers' perception, current use, and future use of computer games in education from a quantitative perspective. The survey was administered by e-mail to selected primary and secondary schools in the countries mentioned and attempted to ensure that a fair selection of teachers from a given school were represented, instead of just a few teachers interested in games from different schools. The survey includes some interesting results, for instance the fact that there is a high level of adaptation of game-based learning among female teachers in the lower grades. Also, the results from the study are encouraging in that it found that teachers are interested in using games; unfortunately, it also discovered that teachers see many barriers to actually engaging in game-based teaching, including a lack of infrastructure and experience. Finally, the survey indicates that we cannot expect that serious games will automatically prevail as younger teachers take over. Young teachers need to settle down and get some experience before they start to use serious games, as the obstacles preventing their use today are very real.

REFERENCES

Abt, C. 1970. *Serious games*. New York: Viking Press.

Bredemeier, M. E., & C. S. Greenblat. 1981. "The educational effectiveness of simulation games: A synthesis of findings." *Simulation & Games* 12(3): 307-331.

Cavallari, J., J. Hedberg, & B. Harper. 1992. "Adventure games in education: A review." *Australian Journal of Educational Technology* 8(2): 172-184.

Cuban, L. 2001. *Oversold and Overused: Computers in the classroom*. Cambridge, MA: Harvard University Press.

de Freitas, S. 2007. "Learning in Immersive Worlds." Joint Information Systems Committee.

Dempsey, J. V., K. Rasmussen, & B. Lucassen. 1996. *The Instructional Gaming Literature: Implications and 99 Sources*. University of South Alabama.

Dorn, D.S. 1989. "Simulation Games: One More Tool On the Pedagogical Shelf." *Teaching Sociology* 17(1): 1-18.

Egenfeldt-Nielsen, S. 2007. *The Educational Potential of Computer Games*. New York: Continuum Press.

IDATE. 2010. *Serious games*, 2nd ed. Digital Home & Entertainment. IDATE, July 2010.

Ito, M. 2008. "Education vs. Entertainment: A Cultural History of Children's Software." In *The Ecology of Games: Connecting Youth, Games, and Learning*, edited by K. Salen. The John D. and Catherine T. MacArthur Foundation Series on Digital Media and Learning. Cambridge, MA: The MIT Press, 89-116.

Leemkuil, H., T. D. Jong, & S. Ootes. 2000. *Review of educational use of games and simulations*. Twente: University of Twente.

Loftus, G. R. & E. Loftus. 1983. *Mind at Play*. Basic Books: New York.

McFarlane, A., A. Sparrowhawk, & Y. Heald. 2002. *Report on the educational use of games*. Teachers Evaluating Educational Multimedia. Cambridge.

McGonigal, J. 2011. *Reality Is Broken: Why Games Make Us Better and How They Can Change the World*. New York: Penguin Press.

McGrenere, J. L. 1996. *Design of Educational Electronic Multi-player Games: A Literature Review*. Vancouver: Department of Computer Science.

Mitchell, A., & C. Savill-Smith. 2004. *The use of computer and video games for learning: A review of the literature*. London: Ultralab: Learning and Skills Development Agency.

Randel, J. M., B. A. Morris, C. D. Wetzel, & B. V. Whitehill. 1992. "The Effectiveness of Games for Educational Purposes: A Review of Recent Research." *Simulation & Gaming* 23(3): 261-276.

Squire, K. 2002. "Cultural Framing of Computer/Video." *Game studies* 1(1).

Van Sickle, R. 1986. "A Quantitative Review of Research on Instructional Simulation Gaming: A Twenty-Year Perspective." *Theory Research in Social Education* 14(3): 245-264.

Wentworth, D. R., & D. R. Lewis. 1973. "A review of research on instructional games and simulations in social studies education." *Social Education* 37: 432-440.

1. STATE OF THE ART

GAME-BASED LEARNING:
A REVIEW OF THE STATE OF THE ART

Patrick Felicia
Simon Egenfeld-Nielsen

1. WHAT IS A DIGITAL VIDEO GAME FOR LEARNING?

1.1 DEFINITION

Although digital video games for learning or with a learning value were already employed in the 1970s (e.g., PLATO: Programmed Logic for Automated Teaching Operations) and 1980s (Greenfield 1984), the term 'digital game-based learning' (DGBL) was made popular by Gee (2003) and Prensky (2001). Game-based learning is a sub-section of serious games, which have mainly come to focus on the educational potential of computer games in the educational system. Prensky (2001) made the claim that the 'digital natives' who were born after 1970 have been exposed to digital devices from a very young age, and have developed skills that need to be acknowledged in schools and universities, notably by engaging and teaching them through video games. According to Prensky (2001), digital natives process information in a significantly different way from previous generations; they multi-task, are used to non-sequential information, and play video games frequently. In contrast, 'digital immigrants' may not have embraced 21st-century literacies, and therefore may find it difficult to reach this new generation of students who speak a rather different language. According to Prensky, there is a gap between these two generations that ought to be bridged. The idea that there could be a cultural and technological divide between these two generations had already been mentioned by other researchers, including Tapscott (1999) and Howe and Strauss (2000), who refer to this generation as the 'net generation' or the 'millennial generation' respectively. According to Tapscott (1999), youths who belong to the 'net generation' are computer savvy and ICT (Information and Communication Technology) literate. As a result, instructional settings should be modified to include a non-linear format, instruction based on discovery, student-centred classes, pedagogical methodologies that encourage the development of meta-cognitive skills rather than asking students to regurgitate information, support for lifelong learning, and personalised teaching strategies.

Prensky's views had many implications for educators, notably that teaching using DGBL could address some of the pitfalls typically found in traditional education (e.g., lack of motivation or confidence). Over the following years the area attracted a lot of attention, with researchers trying to produce scientific evidence in line with Prensky's claims, notably Gee (2003), Squire (2004), and Schaffer (2006). Prensky's views have become more nuanced over the years and are supported by well-established educational theories which promote a constructivist approach to learning, whereby students are actively involved in the learning process and take responsibility for their own learning. One of the main reasons for using GBL is that video games are inherently engaging and intrinsically motivate players to learn and progress accordingly (Malone 1982, Bowmann 1982, Provenzo 1991). They immerse players in a state of flow (Csikszentmihalyi 1990) in which they are motivated to solve problems and overcome challenges. The state of flow may in turn have a positive impact on learning (Webster et al. 1993, Kiili 2005). Video games also seem to increase players' self-efficacy (Toprac 2011), which in turn may increase their academic achievements. Overall, research shows that games can replace the feelings of fear or anxiety felt by students in traditional settings with a desire to play, learn, and succeed (Gillipsie et al. 2010, Tüzün et al. 2009).

Prensky's views have been criticised over the years, as studies revealed that not all teenagers are heavy gamers or even highly proficient at digital skills. The concept of 'digital natives' may need to be further refined, as it appears that there could be "as much variation within the digital natives generation as between generations" (Bennett et al. 2008). This view was also echoed by Pivec (2009), who argues that "Prensky's theories get quoted [...] even when Prensky himself has offered himself no empirical evidence". Pivec (2009) states that today's students may not use technology any differently from their teachers, but instead that technology may be "more appealing to creative learners". According to her, it is game-based teaching rather than GBL that will help to leverage the educational and motivational potential of video games, as instructors play a crucial role in the learning process. The increased focus on the teacher's role is also discussed in a chapter of this book (Hanghøj, in this book). Nonetheless, although Prensky's claim might not be generalisable to all digital natives, his early publications raised a new awareness amongst researchers and educationalists, and promoted the use of video games for learning purposes. Since the terms 'digital natives' and 'digital immigrants' were coined, research in GBL has increased, flourished, and produced a significant body of evidence on the learning and motivational benefits of digital video games. The beginning of the Serious Games movement was marked by the Woodrow Wilson International Centre for Scholars, which launched an initiative aimed at tackling issues such as policy and management. Subsequently, additional groups emerged to investigate social issues, social changes (Games for Change), and health. One of the early research initiatives on serious games was led by MIT's education arcade. This research group focused on creating and assessing novel and engaging video games for learning. During this initiative, games such as Supercharged (Squire et al. 2004b) and Revolution, which featured highly immersive 3D technology to teach physics and history, were created. Since then, the Serious Games movement has spawned additional streams that focus on more specific aspects of DGBL (e.g., Games for Change).

Although further efforts are needed to promote a wider use of DGBL, this medium is now employed across the world in primary schools, secondary schools, universities, and industry. Several challenges still remain for DGBL, including the need for more rigorous empirical evidence on its effectiveness (Van Eck 2006), training teachers (Becker 2007), overcoming practical barriers in school settings (Egenfeldt-Nielsen 2004), as well as further research on the possible negative effects such as addiction or violence that video games may have on players (Escobar-Chaves & Anderson 2008).

1.2 HOW IS DGBL EMPLOYED?

DGBL has been used to teach, train, and raise students' awareness. In schools, it is employed as an adjunct to traditional methodologies to teach mathematics (Kuo & Chong 2009), science (Pajares & Graham 1999), engineering (Coller & Scott 2009), history (Watson et al. 2011, Abrams 2009), and languages (Yip & Kwan 2006). Teachers may use this medium to illustrate concepts and ideas introduced in formal classes, and give students the opportunity to further their knowledge, obtain a deeper understanding of the topic, and practise skills repeatedly until they become proficient (Gillespie et al. 2010). In ideal situations, DGBL interventions include briefing and debriefing sessions conducted by teachers. The latter was proven to increase educational benefits as it makes implicit links between the learning objectives and the game, requiring students to relate to their experience, link their findings to the curriculum, and contextualise their experience (Watson et al. 2011). DGBL is also employed in settings where students are required to create an educational video game. This usually requires students to gather, analyse, and synthesise facts and other relevant information. In this particular case, DGBL not only increases knowledge of the topic, but it also improves students' digital (or 21st-century) skills such as media production (e.g., graphics, audio) and literacy (e.g., reading or writing), as well as other highly transferable skills including collaboration and communication (Beavis & O'Mara 2010).

In industry, DGBL is employed to train staff for situations that would be dangerous or impractical to reproduce otherwise. These DGBL environments are usually highly immersive and have been employed for fire-fighters (Backlund et al. 2007), surgeons (Mann et al. 2002), soldiers (Raybourn 2011), and leaders (Karrasch et al. 2009). DGBL is also used for medical purposes including rehabilitation (Betker et al. 2007), whereby patients are either motivated to perform rehabilitation exercises, or obtain (and consequently be reassured by) more information about their condition through a video game (Kato et al. 2008).

DGBL may also be used to raise awareness and make a social impact. For example, Games for Change (G4C) focus on sensitive issues to address worldwide concerns such as human rights, economics, public policies, public health, poverty, environment, global conflicts, and politics. In this instance, digital games have the advantage of being widely accessible through the Internet, and present a problem that players can appreciate from different perspectives. By taking part in the game, players gain a deeper understanding of the intricacies of the situations depicted in the game, and empathise with the characters (Buch & Egenfeldt-Nielsen 2006).

While DGBL combines the motivational and educational potentials of video games, this can sometimes result in 'Shavian reversals' and create games that are neither fun nor educational (Van Eck 2006). Some researchers are therefore observing and analysing how players learn in video games, to identify how modern classrooms can mirror the learning mechanisms that occur in digital games.

2. WHAT CHARACTERISES DIGITAL GAMES FOR LEARNING?

2.1 GENERAL CHARACTERISTICS

When they are specifically created for learning, digital games usually include some or all of these features: a game format, educational objectives, multimodal representations (e.g., tactile, auditory, or visual), feedback mechanisms (e.g., formative or summative), information provided to users, tools to track users' knowledge and proficiency, and adaptive pedagogical mechanisms. Digital games for learning usually employ visual representations; however, some also account for people with impaired vision, auditory impairment, learning disabilities, or physical disabilities. For example, to accommodate people with impaired vision, several commercial video games employ non-visual cues to transmit information including force-feedback or audio. For people with auditory impairment, closed captioning can be employed to display text on-screen, including descriptions of non-speech elements.

2.2 DGBL: HARDWARE AND SOFTWARE CHARACTERISTICS

Digital games for learning can be employed on a wide range of hardware including desktop computers, game consoles, and handheld devices. The latter is often referred to as Mobile Game-Based Learning (MGBL). In addition to adaptations of titles already available for desktop computers, digital games on mobile devices, due to their location-aware features, can be developed for Augmented Reality (AR) and location-based activities. In AR, the handheld device is employed to provide additional information on the real environment. For example, as students visit a museum, they may obtain information on a particular artefact through their mobile phone. Projects including AR for learning can take the form of treasure hunts, scientific enquiries, or exploration (Klopfer & Squire 2008).

DGBL is also employed on video game consoles. Some popular titles commercialised for these consoles, although they are essentially for entertainment, were found to have an educational value or to promote health (Nitz et al. 2010). Experiments assessing how DGBL can be deployed on video games consoles have used either commercial or bespoke games (Miller & Robertson 2010, Ho et al. 2009).

DGBL can use single- or multi-player games (e.g. MMORPGs), and evidence has demonstrated that the latter is particularly effective for learning as it fosters and leverages collaboration amongst participants (Dickey 2007). However, single-player video games, when they allow players to compare their achievements, may appeal to competitive gamers and motivate them to outdo their peers (Miller & Robertson 2010).

Digital games for learning feature both 2D and 3D technologies. The latter has the advantage of immersing the player and therefore increasing engagement. It is particularly efficient for topics based on investigation and discovery. DGBL applications can be standalone or available online, usually using Java or Flash technologies. DGBL can be implemented in many different game genres including shooters (or 'shoot 'em ups'), bat-and-ball games, platformers, puzzles, mazes, sport games, racing games, Real Time Strategy (RTS), Role Playing Games (RPGs), First-Person Shooters (FPS), Massively Multiple Online Role Playing Games (MMORPGs), educational versions of existing games, and adventure games (see Felicia (2009) for a list of games used for education).

3. TOOLS EMPLOYED TO DESIGN AND DEVELOP DGBL

3.1 DGBL: GAMING TECHNOLOGY

The emergence of DGBL has been facilitated by cheaper and more accessible gaming technology. Current game development tools make it possible to create video games with no or little knowledge of programming. These software comprise game engines, Mods, virtual worlds, and virtual worlds for learning.

Game engines contain all relevant tools for the creation of video games. They include level editors, character animation, preview of the game, scripting, or drag-and-drop features. They can be either 2D (e.g., Adobe Flash, Microsoft Silverlight, or game-maker[1]) or 3D (e.g., Microsoft XNA, Shockwave3D, Unity3D,[2] or Torque Engine[3]). Some game engines are particularly designed for the deployment of educational or training material (e.g., Thinking Worlds[4]). Other game engines may be specifically designed to encourage students to create a video game, using either scripting or drag-and-drop features (e.g., MissionMaker,[5] Alice,[6] Kodu,[7] Scratch,[8] or Quandary[9]).

A 'Mod' is a modification of an existing video game. 'Moding' is a hobby for many gamers, as it gives them the opportunity to modify or extend the lifespan of their favourite video game using a Software Development Kit (SDK) provided by the game publishers. It is often very practical to use Mods for DGBL, as the SDK includes a wide range of tools that speed-up

---

1   http://www.yoyogames.com
2   http://www.unity3d.com
3   http://www.garagegames.com
4   http://www.thinkingworlds.com
5   http://www.immersiveeducation.eu/index.php/missionmaker
6   http://www.aliceprogramming.net
7   http://fuse.microsoft.com/project/kodu.aspx
8   http://www.scratch.mit.edu
9   http://www.halfbakedsoftware.com/quandary.php

the development process. However, the genre of the educational game created with a Mod is usually tied to the genre of the original game (e.g., FPS or RPG). Mods have been used for educational and motivational purposes, including science and employment skills (Brown et al., 2009)

DGBL can be created or derived from existing Multi-User Virtual Environments (MUVEs). MUVEs are virtual environments, usually based on 3D technologies, that enable players to interact in 3D virtual spaces, socialise, create artefacts, and explore. For example, Second Life (SL), an environment that is primarily built for entertainment purposes, has been employed for education (e.g., virtual classes). Sloodle is a particularly interesting application of SL:[10] it is an environment that combines the benefits of Second Life (SL) and Moodle, a Learning Management System (LMS). For example, Sloodle has been employed to teach students remotely (Livingston & Bloomfield 2010). Sloodle makes it possible for instructors to track students' progress and knowledge, while offering an immersive and engaging environment to players. SL employs its own scripting language and makes it possible for developers to create customised interaction mechanisms. More online learning environments are available for educators and designers to customise content based on learning objectives; these environments can be commercial or available for free. For example, Barab et al. (2009) have developed a project called *River City*, a MUVE employed to teach scientific enquiry and 21st-century skills. *River City* is based on *Active World*, a commercial MUVE, and it has been extremely successful in helping teachers promote scientific enquiry amongst students, improving both learning outcomes and students' motivation.

Although some of the solutions mentioned above are free, some cost-effective solutions can also be used to deploy DGBL. These include ARGS (Alternate Reality Games) and games developed using office software such as PowerPoint or Excel, which employ technologies and software already available in most instructional settings.

Digital games may be used depending on the learning outcomes you are aiming to obtain. Learning outcomes usually determine the type of digital game selected. While some games promote surface learning, others are better suited for science as they require students to engage in scientific enquiries, and elaborate and test hypotheses. For example, scrolling shooters can be used to teach mathematic tables or spelling, which are required at

---

10 http://www.sloodle.org

primary and secondary levels. However, for further education, during which students are required to develop higher-level thinking skills and a more comprehensive and subtle understanding, this format may not be suitable. In this case, the video game genres mentioned above may be inappropriate and RPGs or games in which students need to program or create additional resources may be preferred. This is the case for history, geography, science, and engineering (Coller & Scott 2009).

3.2 DGBL: EDUCATIONAL FEATURES

Pinpointing the characteristics of game-based learning is tricky as many of the features overlap with other learning formats, especially the broader idea of eLearning. An important part of making game-based learning function properly is inherited from eLearning, most noticeably, the entire tracking and feedback systems.

Digital games for learning usually encompass mechanisms to track users' knowledge, ensure that they learn accordingly, and trigger interventions when necessary. Most of these mechanisms are based on Intelligent Tutoring Systems (ITSs). ITSs are usually linked to a Learning Management System (LMS), a server that stores students' progress, so that instructors can track this information accordingly and provide help where and when it is needed. ITSs have been employed for many decades; they include four essential components: the student model, the expert model, the pedagogical model, and the interface model. The student model records information pertaining to the student's knowledge, misconceptions, and common mistakes. The expert module includes the knowledge that students may attain upon mastery. The pedagogical model includes appropriate pedagogical strategies to adapt to students' knowledge. The interface model determines how the information is displayed to students. There is a constant communication between these components so that (1) information is gathered from students, (2) knowledge is assessed, (3) appropriate pedagogical strategies are applied, and (4) the information is displayed accordingly. One of the main challenges for the design of ITS systems is to provide assistance to students only when required; this is often referred to as a 'just-in-time' intervention. There is a wide range of 'intelligences' for ITSs, from scripted answers to advanced adaptive strategies. Whilst most ITSs were initially focused on cognition, they have evolved to account for users' behavioural patterns (e.g., attention, emotions, engagement, and boredom). Some recent advancements in video games make it possible to adapt the game-play to users' behaviours and personal characteristics, and provide a more engaging and entertaining experience. Digital games for learning that dynamically adapt to players and maximise learning and motivation are currently being investigated by researchers. Evidence has shown that such mechanisms have the potential to increase the effectiveness of DGBL (Virvou et al. 2005, Marty & Carron 2011, Staalduinen 2011).

It is clear that the above features hold great potential, but one can question whether they are really the core of educational features in game-based learning. The only feature that really sets games apart from other learning areas is the tight focus on creating a conflict (or a problem) that needs to be resolved. This is combined with the game's knack for balancing rewards and feedback systems through sub-goals that makes the learning challenge just right. This is what game designers have been practising and refining for years. When we harness this potential in a way so learning becomes part of this, we see truly engaging game-based learning.

4. WHY CONSIDER GBL COMPARED TO OTHER TRADITIONAL METHODS?

4.1 WHEN IS IT BEST TO USE GBL?

Although video games cannot replace teachers, researchers have found that games can be employed, in specific circumstances, to increase learning outcomes compared to other media or teaching methods, such as textbooks or web-based learning. As suggested by Hays (2005), who conducted a comprehensive literature review of the advantages and limitations of GBL, the benefits brought by video games may be applicable only in specific situations, and games are not the preferred mode of instruction in all cases. Hays (2005) found that video games are more effective when they are incorporated within instructional programmes that include debriefing and feedback, and that instructional support during play may increase the effectiveness of GBL. The effectiveness of debriefing in teaching and training environments has been advocated for over thirty years in simulation research (Lederman 1992, Petranek et al. 1992, Peters & Vissers 2004, Crookall 2010). Games should be used as adjuncts, not as standalone applications, and combined with relevant pedagogies (Hays 2005, Shaffer 2006). As indicated by Wainess (2007) and Dickey (2003), games on their own may not always promote motivation or learning; instead, they need to be considered within GBL practices, and attention should be paid to the environment, rather than the game itself. Support and guidance from the teacher are also crucial for the integration and successful use of video games (Mayer & Bekebreda 2006).

4.2 IMPORTANT FEATURES IN GBL SYSTEMS AND SETTINGS

According to Becker (2006), games are educational and can maintain players' attention for extended periods of time. Video games inherently employ relevant and well-known educational principles (Gee 2007), supporting all five learning capabilities defined by Gagne and Briggs (1972): motor skills, attitude, verbal information, cognitive strategy, and intellectual skills. Gagne's nine events of instruction (1981) can also be identified in the general structure of video games. Video games have proven to be an ideal tool for supporting teaching methods, increasing motivation, and providing a medium that taps into constructivist theories. Compared to traditional teaching methods, games often seem to give students more motivation to learn. In terms of learning outcomes, they are effective in developing a wide range of cognitive skills, including procedural knowledge, declarative knowledge, and higher thinking skills (Kim et al. 2009, Price 2008). Video games may take the form of practice drills (Gillipsie et al. 2010) or quests (Squire & Barab 2004), in which users are required to conduct scientific enquiries. While the evaluation of the former is relatively easy, the latter often raises issues, as it is difficult to evaluate students' higher thinking skills or domain knowledge. This being said, some scientists have successfully employed evaluation tools such as concept maps to measure students' degree of expertise (Coller & Scott 2009). This would apply, for example, to video games featuring open-ended environments where users can experiment, learn from their mistakes, and update their internal 'knowledge map' accordingly. Such environments are especially conducive to the improvement of higher thinking skills required in third-level education; however, because of their open-ended nature, these games, unless they have already been developed commercially, could involve high development costs and therefore dissuade educators and developers from using and developing them. Video games are especially efficient at engaging students, promoting an interest in and a positive behaviour toward the topic, and consequently increasing their knowledge. In particular cases, video games may be more efficient than pen-and-paper methods, because the electronic format enables students to repeat tasks indefinitely and consequently learn from their mistakes through a process of trial and error. Some video games, such as MMORPGs (Massively Multiplayer Online Role Playing Games), are based on collaboration between players, and may therefore be more appropriate and effective for collaboration-based activities. Video games are often developed with flexibility and portability in mind; they can be employed and deployed ubiquitously, inside or outside the classroom, and may therefore offer more opportunities for learning. An additional advantage of video games is that they feature most of the Web 2.0 technologies already employed in schools and universities, including Instant Messaging (IM), video, and web content. Some forms of games, such as ARGs (Alternate Reality Games), which combine the technologies already employed in most educational settings, may offer a cost-efficient solution for GBL development (Hainey et al. 2011). As will be described in the following sections, video games promote digital literacies, especially for students who are required to combine different information sources such as text, audio, or graphics to create an educational game.

5. EMPIRICAL EVIDENCE

5.1 INTRODUCTION

Researchers have conducted controlled studies to explore the motivational and learning advantages of using video games in comparison to more traditional educational environments. Evidence for the advantage of GBL over traditional educational settings presented in the following sections is based on both qualitative and quantitative data, and has been collected using a wide range of methods and techniques including pre- and post-tests, interviews with students and teachers, recordings of students during game play, and focus groups. In the light of the literature, it appears that settings incorporating video games are often more engaging and educationally effective than those that do not include video games.

GBL can be better than traditional teaching methods at improving learning and motivation for a wide range of topics including mathematics (Sorensen & Meyer 2007), physics (Squire et al. 2004b), software engineering (Navarro & Hoek 2007), languages (Yip & Kwan 2006, Miller & Hegelheimer 2006, Neville et al. 2009), history (Abrams 2009, Watson et al. 2011), literature (Stevens 2000) rehabilitation (Adavovich et al. 2003), fire fighting (Chuang & Chen 2009), digital skills (Beavis & O'Mara 2010), mechanical engineering (Coller & Scott 2009), healthy eating (Serrano 2004), algebra (Kebritchi et al. 2010), geography (Virvou et al. 2005), and reading comprehension (Bransford & Schwartz 1999).

5.2 GENERAL BENEFITS COMPARED WITH TRADITIONAL TEACHING

Research has demonstrated that video games, compared to traditional teaching methods, strengthen students' knowledge, skills, and attitudes towards the topic taught (Serrano 2004), and that a game-based learning approach is more motivating and educationally effective (Barab &Warren et al. 2009a), especially for students with poor pre-test scores. GBL is often more effective than conventional educational software, such as web-based software or Computer-Assisted-Instruction (CAI) (Virvou et al. 2005, Papastergiou 2009, Chuang & Chen 2009). In some cases, the educational effectiveness of the game can be improved by customised mechanisms such as pedagogical agents and Intelligent Tutoring Systems (Conati & Zhao 2004).

Students are significantly more engaged when experiencing GBL compared to traditional teaching. They usually find the medium much more enjoyable (Toprac 2011, Vogel et al. 2006), and, in some cases, students can be more focused and disciplined than in web-based instruction settings (Papastergiou 2009). GBL improves students' self-efficacy (Toprac 2009) and can be more efficient than traditional methods for rehabilitation. This was illustrated by Adavovich et al. (2003), who explain that attention, reward, progression, complexity, and skill acquisition are critical to produce improvements in neural structures and functions. They found that virtual reality and video games, because they include all these features, are a suitable tool, especially for the new "MTV generation", who would be well-suited to video game-based therapy.

Students following a game-based approach are able to test their knowledge and refine their understanding of the concepts they have learnt previously. Teachers often notice a change in the behaviours of these students. Amongst other noted benefits, games may be better than paper-based teaching because students can complete exercises repeatedly, with increasing difficulty and challenges. They develop a sense of collaboration or competition between players (Lee et al. 2004, Miller & Robertson 2010b). Games often help students to become more perseverant, and it was suggested that they could be used as an additional resource to palliate teachers' lack of contact hours (Yip & Kwan 2006).

Abrams (2009) conducted a particularly interesting study with three students who underperformed academically and found it difficult to be engaged in traditional educational settings. The study showed that when students were exposed to video games related to the history lesson, they manage to understand concepts by playing the video game. Their gaming experience enriched their understanding of the Second World War by providing them with more vivid details of the battles. The results of the study showed how video games can provide a meaningful context and an interactive visual representation that make the learning material "accessible, useful and relevant", especially for students who tend to be less engaged in more traditional settings. The video game helped them to memorise concepts more vividly because they were contextualised within the game.

5.3 LEARNING BY CREATING A GAME

In addition to using video games for learning, teachers can also require students to create their own games. The instructional approach and didactic underpinnings of this process are different from other types of game-based learning. The student actually constructs the game and therefore their own learning experience much more openly than in most game-based learning titles that are brought to market. Seymour Papert saw a huge potential in this approach to learning games, relating to his theory on constructivist learning (Papert 1980, 1998).

Evidence has demonstrated that this type of creative activity tends to increase students' motivation, their knowledge of the topic, 21st-century literacy skills, and collaborative skills. Learning by creating educational video games places students in an environment that emulates typical computer-supported collaborative environments and might therefore be highly beneficial for developing transferable skills. Several experiments have been conducted using this approach and results have been very encouraging. For example, Beavis & O'Mara (2010) explain how students who created a video game using Game Maker, a free game engine, developed their digital skills. The classroom emulated a working environment in which students collaborated whilst developing their research skills. They engaged with communities in order to find solutions to some of the problems they encountered while developing their game. The social aspects of the classes played a key role in the success of the project. This included praise from the teacher, the pairing of students, and sharing the game with and obtaining feedback from an online community. These "wall-less" classrooms, where students are motivated to create and share information, seem to be conducive to learning. Similar findings were discovered by Maloney et al. (2008), who employed a piece of software called *Scratch* to introduce programming to youths in south central Los Angeles. *Scratch* is a programming environment and language aimed at novice programmers who can use it to create animated stories, games, and interactive presentations. Maloney et al. (2008) found that *Scratch* engaged youths and helped them to discover and use programming commands, sometimes with no guidance from instructors. They believe that this success was due to the relative simplicity of *Scratch*, but also to the social structure in the computer clubhouse where the young people used the program: although instructors had no prior knowledge of the software, they were very encouraging, and it seems that there was an "equitable relationship that turned both mentees and mentors into learners". Maloney et al. (2008) explain that children need to share their projects with others, which may explain the success of the *Scratch* website, where *Scratch* users can upload and share their projects with others.

5.4 HOW IS ENGAGEMENT CHARACTERISED IN GBL ENVIRONMENTS?

Increased engagement in GBL environments is often characterised by students' interactions and discussions outside the classroom. This can be explained by the fact that typical methods teachers use to engage students (e.g., humour, questions, analogies, etcdo not always work, probably because teachers are at the centre of the activity and that the traditional setup of the classroom (e.g., desks lined up in rows and the teacher at the front of the class) is not student-centred. In contrast to common traditional classes, settings using GBL in which students play or create video games can be more conducive to user-centred and collaborative learning. For example, while some team members may play the game, the other members can discuss strategy and provide suggestions. As suggested by Watson et al. (2011), this type of setting promotes interaction within and between teams, and because the teacher is not the centre of instruction, this can result in a more engaging experience. These settings, usually referred to as "wall-less classrooms" are effective because they emulate authentic computer-supported collaborative working environments, allowing students to collaborate, develop their knowledge-finding skills, and engage with communities in order to find solutions to some of the problems they may encounter (Beavis & O'Mara, 2010).

5.5 CONDITIONS FOR SUCCESSFUL INTEGRATION

Researchers often indicate that while playing games is increasingly a part of what it means to be literate in the 21st century, this is not always acknowledged in traditional educational settings. As a result, teaching practices need to be modified in order to account for the digital literacies that are developed outside schools.

Most studies referred to in this chapter suggest that educational benefits are increased when the students have had prior exposure to the topic being taught, with the game providing an opportunity to put learned knowledge into practice (Navarro & Hoek 2007). It also appears crucial that, in the case of bespoke educational video games, students be included in the development process, and introduced to new or unfamiliar game mechanics through a training module. Neville et al. (2009) advise that in-game training (e.g., demo levels or feedback) be complemented with class training sessions, and that attention be paid to contemporary games for affordance, with which students would be familiar and which they would expect in a game (e.g., same quality as commercial games). Providing well-known control schemes may facilitate the learning curve and consequently improve the students' overall experience. Finally, Owston et al. (2009) advise that students should not be involved in collaborative activities (e.g., playing or designing a game) for more than forty-five consecutive minutes, otherwise their productivity may decrease significantly.

5.6 DGBL: BEST PRACTICES

Evidence has shown that while the structure of an educational video game is partly responsible for students' achievements, teachers play an even greater role in the successful implementation of DGBL (Dickey 2003, Hays 2005, Shaffer 2006). In DGBL, games are used as adjuncts to teaching, and teachers usually leverage this medium to engage students and support deeper learning. Teachers and parents are encouraged to develop their gaming literacy and become aware of the opportunities that this medium can offer. Teachers usually need to identify suitable games for their classrooms, test them, ensure that the content is adapted to students' knowledge and cognitive development, explain the game, explain the purpose of the class to students, help students during the game, and organise a debriefing session where links can be established between learning objectives and the game. Although players may learn significant amounts by playing an educational video game, debriefing sessions help to contextualise their knowledge, allow the exchange of information between students, and support constructive discussions. Teachers can assist students with the game mechanics, answer any questions they may have, and ask questions that require students to demonstrate a thorough understanding of the topic.

5.7 POSSIBLE ISSUES AND CONCERNS

Although many educators have embraced the concept of DGBL, several concerns need to be addressed, especially those related to the potential negative effects that video games may have on particularly vulnerable individuals (e.g., addiction and violent behaviours). Although it is agreed that more research needs to be conducted on the links between playing video games and both addiction and violence (Escobar-Chaves & Anderson 2008, Anderson et al. 2010), it is agreed that these symptoms might be more prevalent among particularly vulnerable youths (Ferguson et al. 2008, Chiu et al. 2004) and that they can be identified, prevented, and managed using simple yet effective actions (Bijvank et al. 2008, Olson et al. 2007, Strasburger et al. 2010).

In addition to understanding the limitations of GBL, both researchers and investors should focus on and account for critical factors (e.g., clear relative advantages, increased compatibility, reduced complexity) that are known to increase the diffusion of this medium in educational settings, based on well-established theories (Egenfeldt-Nielsen 2010).

5.8 IMPROVING GBL RESEARCH

Many early studies on GBL were significantly flawed and their results were therefore not generalisable due to researcher bias, short exposure time, and the lack of control groups and integration with previous research (Egenfeldt-Nielsen 2004). This issue has been increasingly addressed over the last few years and more studies now include a rigorous and valid experimental design. This being said, researchers need to ensure that they ask the hard questions concerning the educational use of computer games, compare computer games to other teaching methods (e.g., web-based acitivities), and take into account possible practical difficulties and barriers linked to the installation and use of GBL solutions compared to traditional teaching (e.g., initial efforts in learning the interface, or setting-up the computers), as suggested by Egenfeldt-Nielsen (2004).

Overall, we need to raise the bar for educational use of computer games and ask under what circumstances we learn and how GBL compares to other learning experiences. It is hardly enough to establish that we learn from computer games, as this is essentially true for any activity we engage in; the real question is: what do computer games offer that set them apart from existing educational practice?

Some of these questions have been answered in recent studies, and the following sections provide examples of studies where experimental design allowed for a better interpretation of GBL research.

5.8.1 GBL vs. web-based learning

Papasterigiou (2009) conducted a study that assessed the motivational and educational aspects of video games for Greek high school students, compared to an equivalent website that did not include gaming aspects. The controlled study involved 88 participants (46 boys and 42 girls), aged 16 years old on average, attending a course on computer science. The game had been developed by the researcher; it complied with Greek high-school CS curriculum and covered basic computer memory concepts. The game was designed based on motivational factors identified by Malone (1980) and Prensky (2001) and consisted of a maze in which the players needed to answer questions in order to progress. The web version included the same content (e.g., quizzes to test knowledge). The results showed that students using the game version showed high levels of engagement and focus, whereas the students from the control group (web content) seemed to be less attentive and engaged by the learning material. The students from the first group were quieter and only occasionally conversed with each other, whereas those using the web portal seemed noisier and in some cases were found initiating conversations with no or little relevance to the educational content. Analysis of the pre-tests showed that both groups had a similar knowledge of the topic, though the boys seemed to have a greater knowledge than the girls. It was found that students who used the video game performed better at the post-test than those who used the web-based content. When asked about their impressions of the learning experience, students from group A (who learnt using the game) found the experience significantly more appealing, educationally fruitful, engaging, effective, and relaxed than those from group B; however, they also mentioned that the game could be improved by using 3D graphics, a greater variety of activities, and more adventure (e.g., more rooms or objects to collect).

5.8.2 Learning mechanical engineering through games

Coller and Scott (2009) explored how game-based learning, applied to mechanical engineering, compared to traditional teaching in terms of motivation and achievement. They employed a modification of an existing video games called Torcs, available under the GNU Public license, and renamed it TIU-Torcs. Students had to write their own C++ program in order to interact with the car (e.g., steering, accelerating, etc.); this program was then combined with the existing library of the NIU-Torcs code. The car simulation then ran in real time, displaying the behaviour of the car. Students used their engineering skills, and had to find information outside the game (e.g., linear algebraic equations, differentiation, etc.) in order to optimise the driving, including the gear changes and trajectory, to obtain the fastest time on the track. Coller and Scott (2009) focused on root finding; they believe that some textbooks, including two of the bestselling books for engineering students, offer "artificial engineering problems" because they have no connection to engineering or science, but that they are instead "math problems disguised in an engineering context". They believe that the process of developing a computer program to steer and drive their car, is authentic, which corresponds to the interests of mechanical engineers, who like to build machines and make them work. In this example, it engaged students in understanding engineering concepts and applying them in a concrete, authentic environment. The root finding process enabled them to determine the best time to change gear, or the 'optimal shift point'. Results showed that, as for many similar experiments, students using a game-based learning approach spent significantly more time studying outside the class than those experiencing traditional teaching. They showed more intrinsic motivation, engagement, and intellectual intensity. Although Coller and Scott (2009) agree that it is difficult to measure the skills acquired using a standard test, they attempted to do this using a concept map, a graphical construction of nodes corresponding to important concepts in a domain, and their relationships. They explain that expertise is not always explained by memory but instead by the way knowledge is organised in the mind, and concept maps, which were originally conceived as a learning tool, can be employed as assessment tools. They "tap into the learners' cognitive structure [...] and reveal the sophistication of these structures". Students were asked to construct a concept map of numerical techniques. The experiment involved 86 undergraduates, split into groups who experienced either game-based teaching or traditional teaching. The students' concept maps were marked, and it was found that although there was no statistical difference at the lowest levels of learning (e.g., number of conceptual chunks/nodes, number of major topic listed, number of numerical techniques per major topic) between the two groups, significant differences were noted for higher levels of learning (e.g., interconnection between concepts). A survey conducted amongst 58 students (22 of whom had followed the game-based numerical methods) before they graduated revealed that those who took the game-based version of the course rated it significantly higher than those who took the traditional version; they also valued their initial programming course more.

5.9 THE GAME AHEAD

Looking into the future, it seems that GBL research is moving beyond proving the effectiveness of games for learning. It will still be valuable to examine more closely under what circumstances good game-based learning occurs, and design tighter studies using control groups, baselines, and larger sample sizes. However, future research will probably be focused on best practices and which environments will give the best motivational and educational results. This requires a much more mature praxis around GBL, and will need to involve careful consideration of the context of use for GBL. It is crucial, therefore, that teachers be a part of this process.. Elsewhere in this anthology we presents the results on teachers' use of computer games, and it is discouraging to see that the main obstacles are not related to GBL per se, but rather the elements that surround it. Teachers consider the lack of computer equipment, the difficulty of installation, and the lack of knowledge as the main obstacles to the use of GBL (Egenfeldt-Nielsen in this book). This suggests that we need to focus on teachers, and the obvious place to do this is during teacher training. DGBL needs to become part of teacher training, so that students can harness and employ this new range of educational tools and strategies when they become teachers. We are beginning to see promising changes in this direction in teacher education facilities, but not all training institutes have adopted GBL. Some are still struggling to obtain a decent ICT platform, and GBL could be a big leap for them, whereas others are looking for new educational tools and methodologies to broaden and enhance teachers' skills.

For this to happen, game-based learning developers will also need to improve the quality of the games designed. This will require more research into what makes a good learning game and how they should be developed. Furthermore, it will also involve finding ways to cross educational boundaries so that game-based learning is not limited to one country's curriculum. If the community can find ways to cross these boundaries, the budgets for developing high quality game-based learning will be suddenly within reach.

REFERENCES

Abrams, S. S. 2009. "A gaming frame of mind: digital contexts and academic implications." *Educational Media International* 46(4): 335-347.

Anderson, C. A. et al. 2010. "Violent video game effects on aggression, empathy, and prosocial behaviour in eastern and western countries: a meta-analytic review." *Psychological Bulletin* 136(2): 151-173.

Backlund, P. et al. 2007. "Sidh – a game based firefighter training simulation." In *11th International Conference on Information Visualization*, 899-907. Zurich.

Barab, S., S. Warren, & A. Ingram-Goble. 2009. "Academic Play Spaces." In *Handbook of Research on Effective Electronic Gaming in Education*, edited by R. Ferdig. Hershey: Idea Group Reference.

Beavis, C. & J. O'Mara. 2010. "Computer games – pushing at the boundaries of literacy." *Australian Journal of Language & Literacy* 33(1): 65-76.

Becker, K. 2007. "Digital game-based learning once removed: teaching trainers." *British Journal of Educational Technology* 38(3): 478-488.

Becker, K., 2006. "Pedagogy in commercial video games." In *Games and Simulations in Online Learning: Research and Development Frameworks*, edited by D. Gibson, C. Aldrich, & M. Prensky. Hershey: Idea Group Reference.

Bennett, S., K. Maton, & K. Kervin. 2008. "The 'digital natives' debate: a critical review of the evidence." *British Journal of Educational Technology* 39(5): 775-786.

Betker, A. L. et al. 2007. "Game-based Exercises for Dynamic Short-Sitting Balance Rehabilitation of People With Chronic Spinal Cord and Traumatic Brain Injuries." *Physical Therapy* 87(10): 1389-1398.

Bijvank, M. N. et al. 2008. "Age and violent-content labels make video games forbidden fruits for youth." *Official journal of the American academy of pediatrics* 123: 870-876.

Bowmann, R. F. 1982. "A Pac-Man theory of motivation. Tactical implications for classroom instruction." *Educational Technology* 22(9): 14-17.

Bransford, J. D. & D. L. Schwartz. 1999. "Rethinking transfer: a simple proposal with multiple implications." *Review of Research in Education* 24(1): 61-100.

Brown, D. et al. 2009. "Game on: Accessible serious games for offenders and those at risk of offending." *Journal of Assistive Technologies* 3(2): 13-25.

Buch, T. & S. Egenfeldt-Nielsen. 2006. "The learning effect of Global Conflict: Palestine." Paper presented at the Media@Terra Conference.

Chiu, S.-I., J.-Z. Lee, & D.-H. Huang. 2004. "Video Game Addiction in Children and Teenagers in Taiwan." *CyberPsychology & Behavior* 7(5): 571-581.

Chuang, T. Y. & W. F. Chen. 2009. "Effect of Computer-Based Video Games on Children: An Experimental Study." *Journal of Educational Technology & Society* 12(2): 1-10.

Coller, B. D. & M. J. Scott. 2009. "Effectiveness of using a video game to teach a course in mechanical engineering." *Computers & Education* 53(3): 900-912.

Conati, C. & X. Zhao. 2004. "Building and evaluating an intelligent pedagogical agent to improve the effectiveness of an educational game." In *Proceedings of the 9th international conference on Intelligent user interfaces*, 6-13. Funchal, Madeira, Portugal: ACM.

Crookall, D. 2010. "Serious Games, Debriefing, and Simulation/Gaming as a Discipline." *Simulation & Gaming* 41(6): 898 -920.

Csikszentmihalyi, M. 1990. *Flow: the psychology of optimal experience*. New York: Harper and Row.

Dickey, M. 2007. "Game design and learning: a conjectural analysis of how massively multiple online role-playing games (MMORPGs) foster intrinsic motivation." *Educational Technology Research and Development* 55(3): 253-273.

Dickey, M. D. 2003." Teaching in 3D: Pedagogical Affordances and Constraints of 3D Virtual Worlds for Synchronous Distance Learning." *Distance Education* 24(1): 105-121.

Egenfeldt-Nielsen, S. 2004. "Practical barriers in using educational computer games." *On the Hori* 12(1): 18-21.

Egenfeldt-Nielsen, S. 2010. "The Challenges to Diffusion of Educational Computer Games." Paper presented at the European Conference on Game-Based Learning, Copenhagen, Denmark, October 21-22, 2010.

Escobar-Chaves, S. L. & C. A. Anderson. 2008. "Media and risky behaviors." *Children and Electronic Media* 18(1): 147-180.

Felicia, P. 2009. *Digital games in schools: a handbook for teachers*. Brussels: European Schoolnet.

Ferguson, C. J. et al. 2008. "Violent Video Games and Aggression: causal relationship or by-product of family violence and intrinsic violence motivation?" *Criminal Justice and Behavior* 35(3): 311-332.

Gee, J. P. 2003. *What video games have to teach us about learning and literacy*. Basingstoke: Palgrave Macmillan.

Gillespie, L., F. Martin, & M. Parker. 2010. *Electronic Journal of Mathematics & Technology* 4(1): 68-80.

Greenfield, P. 1984. *Mind and Media*. Cambridge, MA: Harvard University Press.

Hainey, T., T. Connolly, & L. Boyle. 2011. "Arguing for multilingual motivation in web 2.0: An evaluation of a large-scale European pilot." In *Improving learning and motivation through educational games: multidisciplinary approaches*, edited by P. Felicia. Hershey: Idea Group Reference.

Hays, R. T. 2005. *The effectiveness of instructional games: a literature review and discussion*. Orlando, Florida: Naval Air Warfare Center Training.

Ho, J. et al. 2009. "Investigating the Effects of Educational Game with Wii Remote on Outcomes of Learning." In *Transactions on Edutainment III*. Lecture Notes in Computer Science. Berlin / Heidelberg: Springer. 240-252. Available at: http://dx.doi.org/10.1007/978-3-642-11245-4_21, accessed on November 1, 2011.

Howe, N. & B. Strauss. 2000. *Millenials rising: the next great generation*. New York: Vintage.

Karrasch, A. et al. 2009. "Using simulation to train influence." Paper presented at the Interservice/Industry Training, Simulation & Education Conference (I/IT SEC), Orlando, Florida, August 18-20, 2009.

Kato, P. M. et al. 2008. "A Video Game Improves Behavioral Outcomes in Adolescents and Young Adults With Cancer: A Randomized Trial." *Pediatrics* 122(2): 305-317.

Kebritchi, M., A. Hirumi & H. Bai. 2010. "The effects of modern mathematics computer games on mathematics achievement and class motivation." *Computers & Education* 55(2): 427-443.

Kiili, K. 2005. "Digital game-based learning: Towards an experiential gaming model." *The Internet and Higher Education* 8(1): 13-24.

Kim, B., H. Park, & Y. Baek. 2009. "Not just fun, but serious strategies: Using meta-cognitive strategies in game-based learning." *Computers & Education* 52(4): 800-810.

Klopfer, E. & K. Squire. 2008. "Environmental Detectives—the development of an augmented reality platform for environmental simulations." *Educational Technology Research and Development* 56(2): 203-228.

Kuo, H. H. & J. Chong. 2009. "Integrating Computer Games with Mathematics Instruction in Elementary School- An Analysis of Motivation, Achievement, and Pupil-Teacher Interactions." In Proceedings of World Academy of Science: Engineering & Technology. 261-263.

Lederman, L. C. 1992. "Debriefing: Toward a Systematic Assessment of Theory and Practice." *Simulation & Gaming* 23(2): 145 -160.

Lee, J. et al. 2004. "More than just fun and games: assessing the value of educational video games in the classroom." In *CHI '04 extended abstracts on Human factors in computing systems*. Vienna, Austria: ACM. 1375-1378.

Livingston, D. & P. R. Bloomfield., 2010. "Mixed-methods and mixed worlds: engaging globally distributed user groups for extended evaluation studies." In *Research Learning in Virtual Worlds*, edited by A. Peachey, J. Gillen, D. Livington, and S. Smith-Robbins. London: Springer. 159-176.

Malone, T. W. 1982. "Toward a theory of intrinsically motivating instruction." *Cognitive Science* 5(4): 333-369.

Maloney, J. H. et al. 2008. "Programming by choice: Urban youth learning programming with scratch." *ACM SIGSE Bulletin – SIGSE 08* 40(1): 367-371.

Mann, B.D. et al. 2002. "The development of an interactive game-based tool for learning surgical management algorithms via computer." *The American journal of surgery* 183(3): 305-308.

Marty, J.-C. & T. Carron. 2011. "Hints for Improving Motivation. In: Game-Based Learning Environments." In *Improving learning and motivation through educational games: multidisciplinary approaches*, edited by P. Felicia. Hershey: Idea Group Reference.

Mayer, I. & G. Bekebreda. 2006. "Serious games and simulation based e-learning for infrastructure management." In *Affective and emotional aspects of human-computer interaction: Emphasis on game-based and innovative learning approaches*, edited by M. Pivec. Amsterdam: IOS Press BV.

Miller, D. J. & D. P. Robertson. 2010. "Using a games console in the primary classroom: Effects of 'Brain Training' programme on computation and self-esteem." *British Journal of Educational Technology* 41(2): 242-255.

Miller, M. & V. Hegelheimer. 2006. "The SIMs meet ESL Incorporating authentic computer simulation games into the language classroom." *Interactive Technology and Smart Education* 3(4): 311-328.

Navarro, E. O. & A. van der Hoek.. 2007. "Comprehensive Evaluation of an Educational Software Engineering Simulation Environment." In *Proceedings of the 20th Conference on Software Engineering Education & Training*, 195-202. IEEE Computer Society.

Neville, D. O., B. E. Shelton, & B. McInnis. 2009. "Cybertext redux: using digital game-based learning to teach L2 vocabulary, reading, and culture." *Computer Assisted Language Learning* 22(5): 409-424.

Nitz, J. C. et al. 2010. "Is the Wii Fit™ a new-generation tool for improving balance, health and well-being? A pilot study." *Climacteric* 13(5): 487-491.

Olson, C. K. et al. 2007. "Factors correlated with violent video game use by adolescent boys and girls." *Journal of adolescent health* 41(1): 77-83.

Owston, R., N. S. Wideman & Christine Brown. 2009. "Computer game development as a literacy activity." *Computers and Education* 53(3): 977-989.

Pajares, F. & L. Graham. 1999. "Self-Efficacy, Motivation Constructs, and Mathematics Performance of Entering Middle School Students." *Contemporary Educational Psychology* 24(2): 124-139.

Papastergiou, M. 2009. "Digital Game-Based Learning in high school Computer Science education: Impact on educational effectiveness and student motivation." *Computers & Education* 52(1): 1-12.

Papert, S. 1980. *Mindstorms: Children, Computers, and Powerful Ideas*. New York: Basic Books.

Papert, S. 1998. "Does Easy Do It? Children, Games and Learning." *Game Developer*.

Peters, V. A. M. & G. A. N. Vissers. 2004. "A Simple Classification Model for Debriefing Simulation Games." *Simulation & Gaming* 35(1): 70 -84.

Petranek, C. F., S. Corey & R. Black. 1992. "Three Levels of Learning in Simulations: Participating, Debriefing, and Journal Writing." *Simulation & Gaming* 23(2): 174-185.

Pivec, P. 2009. "Game-based learning or game-based teaching." Available at: http://webarchive.nationalarchives.gov.uk/20101102103654/emergingtechnologies.becta.org.uk/index.php?section=etr&rid=14692, accessed February 19, 2010.

Prensky, M. 2001. "Digital natives, digital immigrants part 1." *On the horizon* 9(5): 1-6.

Price, C. B. 2008. "The usability of a commercial game physics engine to develop physics educational materials: An investigation." *Simulation & Gaming* 39(3): 319-337.

Provenzo, E. F. 1991. *Video Kids: Making sense of Nintendo*. Cambridge, MA: Harvard University Press.

Raybourn, E. 2011. "Honing emotional intelligence with game-based crucible experiences." *International Journal of Game-Based Learning* 1(1): 32-44.

Serrano, E. S. 2004. "The evaluation of food pyramid games, a bilingual computer nutrition education program for latino youth." *Journal of Family and Consumer Sciences Education* 22(1).

Shaffer, D. W. 2006. *How computer games help children learn*. New York: Palgrave Macmillan.

Sorensen, B. & B. Meyer. 2007. "Serious Games in language and learning – a theoretical perspective." In *Digital Games Research Association 2007 Conference: Situated Play*, 559-566 Tokyo, September 24-28 2007

Squire, K. & S. Barab. 2004. "Replaying history: engaging urban underserved students in learning world history through computer simulation games." In *Proceedings of the 6th international conference on Learning Sciences*, 505-512. Santa Monica, California. International Society of the Learning Sciences.Squire, K., M. Barnett et al. 2004b. "Electromagnetism supercharged!: learning physics with digital simulation games." In *Proceedings of the 6th international conference on Learning sciences*, 512-520 Santa Monica, California. International Society of the Learning Sciences.Staalduinen, J.-P. 2011. "A First Step Towards Integrating Educational Theory And Game Design." In *Improving learning and motivation through educational games: multidisciplinary approaches*, edited by P. Felicia. Hershey: Idea Group Reference.

Stevens, D. A. 2000. "Leveraging technology to improve test scores: a case study of low-income hispanic students." Paper presented at the International Conference on Learning with Technology, Temple University, Philadelphia. Available at: http://www.lexialearning.com/files/tornillo.pdf, accessed on November 1, 2011.

Strasburger, V. C., A. B. Jordan & E. Donnerstein. 2010. "Health effects of media on children and adolescents." *Official journal of the American academy of pediatrics* 125(4): 756.

Tapscott, D. 1999. "Educating the Net Generation." *Educational Leadership* 56(5): 6-11.

Toprac, P. 2011. "Motivating by design: an interesting digital-game based learning environment." In *Improving learning and motivation through educational games: multidisciplinary approaches*, edited by P. Felicia. Hershey: Idea Group Reference.

Tüzün, H. et al. 2009. "The effects of computer games on primary school students' achievement and motivation in geography learning." *Computers & Education* 52(1): pp. 68-77.

Van Eck, R. 2006. "Digital game-based Learning: It's not just the digital natives who are restless." *EDUCAUSE Review* 41(2).

Virvou, M., G. Katsionis & K. Manos. 2005. "Combining software games with education: Evaluation of its educational effectiveness." *Educational Technology & Society* 8(2): 54-65.

Vogel, J. J. et al. 2006. "Computer gaming and interactive simulations for learning: a meta-analysis." *Journal of Educational Computing Research* 34(3): 229-243.

Wainess, R. 2007. "The potential of games & simulations for learning and assessment." In *2007 CRESST Conference: The Future of Test-based Educational Accountability*. Los Angeles, California, January, 22 2007.

Watson, W. R., C. J. Mong & C. A. Harris. 2011. *A case study of the in-class use of a video game for teaching high school history.* Available at: http://search.ebscohost.com/login.aspx?direct=true&db=aph&AN=55056983&site=ehost-live, accessed on September 14th 2011.

Webster, J., L. K. Trevino & L. Ryan. 1993. "The dimensionality and correlates of flow in human-computer interactions." *Computers in Human Behavior* 9(4): 411-426.

Yip, F. W. M. & A. C. M. Kwan. 2006. "Online vocabulary games as a tool for teaching and learning English vocabulary." *Educational Media International* 43(3): 233-249.

2. METHODS

2 A. DESIGN-BASED ACTION RESEARCH

Rikke Magnussen & Birgitte Holm Sørensen

1. INTRODUCTION

The debate about the learning potential of games has been going on for the past thirty years; in recent years it has resulted in a boost of both academic research interest and the development of game formats (Gee 2005, Squire & Klopfer 2007, Shaffer 2007, Magnussen 2008, Hanghøj 2008). Numerous educational computer games are available for today's teachers, but studies show that the implementation of computer games in everyday teaching is often problematic (Egenfeldt-Nielsen 2004). This focus on designing and implementing game-based learning environments in educational settings implies a need to rethink methodological questions on how to apply and study educational designs and their relation to learning processes. Thus, there is a growing need to rethink methodological approaches in order to produce the appropriate tools to map and explore the complexity of contexts and to understand how, when, and why learning takes place in game-based educational settings. In this chapter, we discuss concrete experiences with design-based research (DBR) and action research as methodological approaches for designing and intervening with educational games or game-inspired learning environments in school education. We present two empirical studies of an educational design involving the game Global Conflict: Latin America in Danish language and geography education in Danish upper secondary schools. The methodological approaches in these two case studies are discussed, and we reflect on how DBR as a methodological approach in game studies can be extended with elements of action research, such as 'participant' integration in the various phases of design.

2. DESIGN-BASED RESEARCH IN STUDIES OF LEARNING GAMES

Design-based research has been described as a methodological approach to developing and generating theory by creating new types of game-based education (Squire 2005, Magnussen 2008, Hanghøj 2008). The design and study of new types of theory-based educational games involve complex processes that challenge existing methodological approaches. These challenges concern both the integration and balancing of game design and research processes in the development of new types of game-based learning spaces and the integration of these designs in educational settings (Ejersbo et al. 2008). In the development of new types of learning games, complex processes of game development and research have to be combined. Commercial edutainment games are often based on traditional instructional theories of learning (Gee 2005). The development of new types of learning games requires knowledge about learning processes and learning theory that educational game researchers can contribute to the development process. Researchers, on the other hand, generally do not share the developers' experience of how to make games with the dynamics, rules, and narratives that modern games possess; and researchers can, therefore, benefit from collaboration with game developers. Another problem is that many existing learning computer games are developed to run independently from the classroom setting and the teacher. Teachers question the learning potential of these games and whether they fulfil curricular goals if they are not integrated in the activities that take place in their educational setting (Hanghøj & Brund 2010).

DBR has been applied as a methodological approach to developing and studying new types of game-based learning environments (see Barab & Squire 2004, Magnussen 2008). This methodological approach combines empirical educational research with theory-driven design of learning environments (Brown 1992, Design-Based Research Collective 2003). Design experiments are, therefore, described both as a method for 'engineering' learning environments and for developing domain-specific theories (Cobb et al. 2003). The design of learning environments and the development of theories of learning are closely intertwined and characteristic for the method, because they occur through continuous cycles of design, enactment, analysis, and redesign. The design scientist's role is to "engineer innovative educational environments and simultaneously conduct experimental studies of those innovations" (Brown 1992, 141). One of the strengths of DBR is its capacity to serve as a framework for combining and integrating various research methods at different phases of research and development (Squire 2005). As a result, the methodological approach is suitable both for engineering learning environments, such as educational games, and for developing domain-specific theories (Cobb et al. 2003). DBR is thus described as an emerging paradigm that "can help create and extend knowledge about developing, enacting, and sustaining innovative learning environments"

(Design-Based Research Collective 2003). Because it is a fairly new research approach, however, there are fundamental discussions going on about the standards for DBR to improve the quality of studies (Dede 2004, Van den Akker et al. 2006).

Action research is an approach that resembles design-based research in some ways. It is practice-oriented and marked by a change in research, analysis, actions, and evaluations. The method intends to contribute to both action and research. It requires collaboration between participant and researcher, which may differ according to what type of action research is applied. Action research is often defined having three sub-directions (Masters 1995, Herr & Anderson 2005), of which only technical action and practical action are relevant for discussion in this instance. Technical action research is characterised by the fact that the starting point is the problem posed by the researcher. The interest here is, e.g., to develop concepts by employing user-involvement. Often, the user is not included until late in the phase. This research approach resembles design-based research in various ways. The intention of practical action research is to create changes in existing systems. In this approach, a close collaboration between the researcher and participant about what is going to be developed takes place (ibid.). Within the pedagogical field, practical action research has been dominant. This is a dialogue-oriented process in which ideas for and the objective of the development of action research and/or alternatives is discussed between researcher and participants and in which the planning of the phases of progression is arranged between the two parties. Design-based research may, to its advantage, derive inspiration from the pedagogical approach of action research not merely by including user participation but by considering participants to a greater extent early in the idea phase and in the determination of objectives. The idea-generation phase is crucial in order to include as many aspects and relations as possible before the first development phase commences. This phase can therefore take account of the experiences the participants may have had within the field.

In this chapter, we present a study of a game-based learning environment in educational settings in Danish school classes, and we discuss what can be learned from the methodological design approach, drawing on elements from DBR and action research. Our interests concern the processes in which the teachers and the students turn the learning technology into a design for educational games that is modelled for the local context – designs which are more 'loose' or 'open' for redesign in the local school culture.

3. CYCLES OF DESIGN AND OBSERVATIONS OF PLAY

The empirical study of Global Conflict: Latin America was conducted in two cycles of problem definition, design, intervention, and analysis. Global Conflicts is an educational game series used for teaching history, citizenship, geography and media courses. The series focuses on different conflicts throughout the world and the underlying themes of democracy, human rights, globalization, terrorism, climate and poverty. The study involved five different teachers and their three classes. In this chapter, we report on the first cycle that was set up as part of a collaboration with the primary game developer Serious Games Interactive. The game developer was interested in gaining knowledge about the setting in which the game was played. The developers had found that teachers could be a barrier to introducing serious games into schools (Egenfeldt-Nielsen 2004), and were therefore interested in understanding how the game could be integrated into different educational settings and, at the same time, provide a different approach to teaching the subjects for which it was designed.

Prior to the first DBR studies, the research group conducted two pilot studies in two 8th grade classes in the Copenhagen area. Both classes were videotaped in the single lesson (of 45 minutes) it takes to play one mission in *i*. The research group had not seen the game in action and was therefore interested in understanding what practices emerge in class when the game was played as part of the processes of learning social science subjects. In the pilot study, we generally saw two types of student practices. The first type was characterised by 'fast players'. Students were sharing computers in groups of two, and the fast player groups would move through the 3D game world at a rapid pace and quickly click on different options. They would typically be able to play through more than one mission in a single school lesson. The second type of player had a slower pace. These students would take time to read through the texts in the game and make choices. They would typically only be able to complete one mission within a lesson. After the sessions, we conducted group interviews with the students and their teachers to record responses both to the game and to how the game related to the educational practices in the school subjects for which it was designed. In these interviews, both students and teachers complained that the game required reading through a lot of text on the screen but also that players could click through the game without reading or understanding the texts. In spite of these negative responses, the game was also considered an interesting educational resource for the subject of geography that could bolster classroom teaching by providing an experience of being in a foreign locality and having to navigate in a foreign culture with different types of problems and actors. The teacher pointed out that the goals and topics of the game needed to be better integrated into the curriculum to prevent it from being reduced to a stand-alone exercise.

This integration became the focal point of the next cycle of DBR studies. The aim in this phase was to redesign the classroom setting for game activities to interact with class activities. The springboard for doing this was a focus on the journalist role. Part of the argumentation for choosing this design was that learning to analyse and write in journalistic genres is an essential part of the Danish language curriculum, and the game already contained a journalist role as well as recommendations for using the game as an inspiration for writing articles in the classroom. The design was refined through a series of what we chose to call 'expert interviews'. In these four interviews, we discussed the Global Conflict game and the journalist role in the game with fellow researchers, a game developer, a game critic at a Danish newspaper, and a teacher at a Danish school of journalism. As a result of these different design considerations and sources of inspiration, we conducted two more rounds of observations with a set-up aimed at expanding the student role as journalist within the game. The students were required to use the experiences and the information gathered within the game to write actual articles that addressed relevant social studies topics. The set-up was planned together with the teachers before each round of observations with the aim of exploring how the redesigned game activities functioned within the teachers' existing educational aims and practices. The four participating teachers had formulated explicit curricular goals for the game activities. The students were not only required to play the game but also to write an article in a chosen journalistic genre based upon their game experience and other available resources – i.e. their geography or social studies textbooks and newspaper articles describing various aspects of the conflict. Moreover, the four teachers also explained how the students' game experience could be related to previous teaching. We conducted 4 – 5 hours of video observations of game-playing and article-writing sessions in two 9th grade classes. We also conducted interviews with students in the different classes and the participating teachers after each of the game sessions.

We observed a variety of responses to the combined game and article scenarios in the two different 9th grade classes; but, as in the first pilot studies, we also generally observed two types of approaches in the game-playing sessions: 1) students who, after initial focused play, would start clicking randomly to get through the game and 2) students who would continue throughout the whole session to take time to read through the texts and make decisions based on what they read. An example of the first type of strategy is provided by two students in Class A who played the game in the school's computer room. At first, they found the 3D environment interesting. They initially played the game by reading through the texts and following instructions, as they collaborated in seeking information about the case they were investigating as 'journalists'. After approximately 15-20 minutes of play, they started to click more randomly through the different options in the game, to lose interest, and to talk to other classmates about unrelated issues. The second example of game play approach was provided by a group of students in another class, Class B. The group played the game by reading through all the texts in the game and discussing options offered in relation to the investigation. The teachers in both classes had suggested that they should take notes while they played the game to support the writing of articles after the game. This note-taking procedure became an established practice in the way the group played the game. Notes were taken from information given in interviews and from background information given in the introduction to the mission. These notes were also used in the writing of articles after the game.

The overall impression of these game sessions was that the game-playing and the article-writing activities became two isolated endeavours. In all the classes we observed, students would first play the game in the school computer room and then go to the classroom to write an article as if they were a journalist returning from the geographic area the game was simulating. Due to factors that may relate to localities in the school and elements of the game design, the school and game activities seemed unrelated. Whereas students were motivated whilst playing the game, we generally saw low motivation in the article-writing sessions in the class, which may stem from the fact that the lack of connection between activities did not create a meaningful educational design.

In the following group interviews with teachers, we first focused on responses to the sessions but also asked teachers for suggestions as to how to develop these game-based educational designs further. One example of a concrete suggestion for integrating the game came from a group of teachers who criticised the game design for rewarding those students who simply clicked frantically through the dialogue boxes and still received a moderate score even though they had only read a small percentage of the text. These students made no notes during the game sessions, which made it difficult for them to write journalistic articles. In response to this, one teacher suggested that the game should actually 'require' the students to make notes during game play, which subsequently were to be used for articles. Another aspect commented on was the role the teachers themselves played in the different types of activities. In the game activities, teachers mainly participated by 'looking over the shoulders' of the students. The game was designed for students to play on their own or in groups of two and did not integrate a teacher role or leave any opening for the teacher to be a part of the game interaction. As an example of other types of games that are designed for teacher interaction, a forensic role-playing game in which the teacher plays the chief investigator was mentioned (Magnussen 2008). The researchers presented the teachers with previous research by the developer that found that teachers can be a barrier to integrating games in school and that, therefore, it might be a better strategy to design games that do not depend on teacher participation because of the technical difficulties this presents to most teachers. To this, the teachers replied that it was simply a question of providing them with a good teacher manual.

Additional studies with a larger group of teachers showed that teachers in general were concerned about how to make the GC game scenarios "visible" in relation to particular curricular aims (Hanghøj & Brund 2010). In these studies, it was also pointed out that the GC games should not stand alone but should be integrated with other learning resources (e.g., film clips, texts on the Internet, student assignments, etc.) and other teaching methods, such as direct instruction or classroom discussions. Several teachers mentioned how the GC games could work as an introduction to a particular theme – e.g., when planning a theme week about the African continent.

4. DISCUSSION AND CONCLUSIONS

In the studies of Global Conflicts: Latin America, we have presented a DBR study of designing an educational game to become part of and create innovative approaches to education in primary language education and geography. The approach was, in collaboration with teachers, to use article activities to create a framework in which to integrate a game that the game company had already finished developing for primary language education. As described above, there were several challenges and barriers in the interplay between the school context and the game design that created difficulties in reaching this goal. Firstly, the article-writing and the game-playing activities became isolated activities, which may be due to the fact that the article-writing activity was not supported by journalistic writing tools such as the note-taking system suggested by one of the teachers. The game-based activities did not include a consistent role for teachers. Because of this, the teacher did not have a clear role in the research aspect of the student's journalistic activities but only in the classroom afterwards, when some students had already gathered the information but others had spent their time clicking randomly through the game. As a result, the design of a journalist framework around the gaming activities did not change the non-reflective approach adopted by some of the students.

We suggest that the problems encountered in this study lie more generally in the approach of seeking to integrate game designs, such as the game Global Conflict: Latin America, that were developed without the participation of the parties that will be using them as part of their educational practices. In the DBR cycles described, the game was first developed by the game company and only then introduced to teachers and students by a team of researchers. We argue that, in this approach, teachers and students are viewed as 'users' and not as parties involved in the development. The teachers took part in designing the educational framework for the game; but, as we have seen, the closed system of the game made it difficult to create structures such as teacher roles and a built-in note-taking system that could connect the game and school activities. This element should be included in future generations of the game, and teachers and, perhaps students should be integrated as 'participants' in the development of these next generations of to suggest structures for further integration of the game into school activities.

But will this approach solve the problem of how to integrate a completed game-based learning design in a school culture? We have argued in this chapter that building an educational framework around a finished product is not sufficient for it to become part of the practice. The game system itself needs built-in openness and flexibility to be able to adapt to the local context and to integrate ostensible 'users' as 'participants' and 'co-designers'. But we still need to consider the design scientist's role in providing innovative practices in school education (Brown 1992). We suggest an approach in which the scope of DBR to "engineer innovative educational environments and simultaneously conduct experimental studies of those innovations" (Brown 1992, 141) is inspired by the concept of 'participants' in pedagogical action research in which the teachers are involved, e.g., in the idea-generation phase and in later development phases. We propose the following model as a description of the methodological approach we are suggesting.

SERIOUS GAMES IN EDUCATION

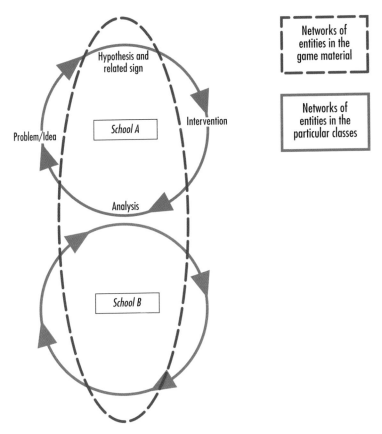

Figure 1: *Design-based participatory research. The model illustrates the redesign conducted by participants from the local school culture when the same game (circle with blue dotted line) is implemented and played in two different educational contexts (Schools A and B). Because of this local redesign the same game can lead to different learning and play practices in the different contexts (black vs. red circle). There will however also be practices that are alike in both settings due to the shared network of game entities (blue dotted circle).*

This model shows how teachers, students, and other entities in a local school culture are integrated as participants in the redesign of game-based learning technology. In this process, the teachers and the students turn the learning technology into a design that is modelled for the local context, which can lead to an integration of educational games as a practice in the local culture. In this methodological approach, users are invited to be participants in the phases of problem definition, design, intervention, and analysis. This process stands in relation to the development of a specific innovative game or game idea introduced from outside the school culture (figure 1 – circle with blue dotted line). With inspiration from an ongoing study of the possibility of implementing game-inspired designs for technology innovation in science education (Magnussen 2010), we suggest collaboration with other types of 'participants' in the early phases of problem definition, design, implementation, and analysis. In this type of participant DBR research, the researcher still has the role of designing and introducing innovative learning designs and technologies into schools. This role is essential as these designs should serve as the researcher's space for experiments and the generation of new knowledge about learning with new technologies. The structure of the design should, however, be kept open to problem definition and design in collaboration with teachers, developers, or other parties with knowledge about the context, subject area, or technology. Inviting these parties in as participants in the modelling of the design may make the process more complex. However, if the participants in a local culture are given the opportunity to identify central problems or elements then they can be taken into consideration in the early prototypes of the design. In the implementation phase, we advocate game designs in which the teacher's role is explicitly designed as part of the game universe. Examples might include roles as the local team leader of a fictional innovation team or as chief investigator in a fictional crime investigation (Magnussen 2008, 2010). In other studies, we have seen that including teachers as game characters makes it possible to change the design 'on the fly' and conduct design experiments when interesting and unexpected situations or challenges arise during observation. The teacher can choose to ask other types of questions or to set up new types of challenges to experiment with new elements of the space of which the design is a part. In the analysis phase, we suggest that teachers or developers should also be invited in as partners in the discussion of results. Presenting teachers and other participants with the results of the analysis or inviting them to participate in publications with the aim of redesign can bring forward different and unanticipated types of questions with regard to the context and school culture, which can be essential for future development and implementation in other contexts.

Generally, we advocate an understanding of the design concept in which finished designs are modelled for users to become 'participants'. Consequently, the structures in these designs have to be more 'loose' or 'open' for redesign in the local school culture. Defining and experimenting with this type of design will provide perspectives for future research.

REFERENCES

Barab, S. & K. Squire. 2004. "Design-based Research: Putting a Stake in the Ground." *Journal of the Learning Sciences* 13(1): 1-14.

Brown, A. 1992. "Design Experiments: Theoretical and Methodological Challenges in Creating Complex Interventions in Classroom Settings." *The Journal of Learning Sciences* 2(2): 141-178.

Cobb, P., J. Confre, A. diSessa, R. Lehrer, & L. Schauble. 2003. "Design Experiments in Education Research." *The Educational Researcher* 32(1): 9-13.

Dede, C. 2004. "If Design-Based Research Is the Answer, What Is the Question?" *Journal of the Learning Sciences* 13(1): 105-114.

Design-Based Research Collective (DBRC). 2003. "Design-based Research: An Emerging Paradigm for Educational Inquiry." *Educational Researcher* 32(1): 5-8.

Egenfeldt-Nielsen, S. 2004. "Practical Barriers in Using Educational Computer Games." *On the Horizon* 12(1): 18-21.

Ejersbo, L. R., R. Engelhardt, L. Frølunde, T. Hanghøj, R. Magnussen, & M. Misfeldt. 2008. "Balancing Product Design and Theoretical Insights." In *Handbook of Design Research Methods in Education: Innovations in Science, Technology, Engineering, and Mathematics Learning and Teaching*, edited by A. E. Kelly, R. A. Lesh, & J. Y. Baek. New York and London: Routledge. 149-165.

Gee, J. P. 2005. "What Would a State of the Art Instructional Video Game Look Like?" *Innovate* 1(6) Available at http://www.innovateonline.info/index.php?view=article&id=80, accessed on April 24, 2008.

Hanghøj, T. & Brund, C. E. 2010. Teacher roles and positionings in relation to educational games. In B. Meyer (Ed.), Proceedings of the 4th European Conference on Games Based Learning European, Copenhagen, Denmark. UK: Academic Publishing Limited, 115-122.

Hanghøj, T. 2011. Playful knowledge: an explorative study of educational gaming. Saarbrücken: Lambert Academic Publishing, 2011.

Mol, A. 2002. *The Body Multiple: Ontology in Medical Practice*. Durham, NC: Duke University Press.

Magnussen, R. 2011. Game-like Technology Innovation Education. *International Journal of Virtual and Personal Learning Environments*, 2(2), pp. 30-39.

Magnussen, R. 2008. "Representational Inquiry in Science Learning Games." PhD Diss., University of Aarhus.

Masters, J. 1995 "The History of Action Research." In *Action Research Electronic Reader*, edited by I. Hughes. The University of Sydney.

Herr, K. & G. L. Anderson. 2005. *The Action Research Dissertation: A Guide for Students and Faculty*. CA: Sage Publications.

Shaffer, D. W. 2007. *How Computer Games Help Children Learn*. New York: Palgrave Macmillan.

Squire, K. & E. Klopfer. 2007. "Augmented Reality Simulations on Handheld Computers." *Journal of the Learning Sciences* 16(3): 371-413.

Squire, K. D. 2005. "Resuscitating Research in Educational Technology: Using Game-Based Learning Research as a Lens for Looking at Design-Based Research." *Educational Technology* 45(1): 8-14.

Van den Akker, J., K. Gravemeiger, S. McKenney, & N. Nieveen. 2006. "Introducing Educational Design Research." In *Educational Design Research*, edited by J. Van den Akker, K. Gravemeiger, S. McKenney, & N. Nieveen. London: Routledge. 1-8.

2 B. MAKING CONNECTIONS – GLOBAL AND LOCAL ISSUES IN RESEARCHING THE POLICY OF SERIOUS GAMES IN EDUCATION

Bente Meyer, Birgitte Holm Sørensen, Thorkild Hanghøj & Lars Birch Andreasen

1. INTRODUCTION

As has been suggested by several recent studies, serious games are notoriously difficult to integrate into formal education (Egenfeldt-Nielsen 2004, 2010, Hanghøj & Meyer 2010, Mayo 2011). The reasons for these difficulties (and indeed the truth of the statement itself) may vary in local contexts. However, the consequences of these barriers for emergent learning technologies like games is that the need for knowledge of and strategies for disseminating games into classroom practices is becoming more urgent. This is especially relevant for serious games developers who need tools for establishing dissemination networks that will engage relevant actors in their products and in game-based learning.

One of the things that affects the distribution of serious games on the formal educational market is the increasingly significant role of policy on national and global educational practice and content. For instance, Merrilea J. Mayo argues, on the basis of an analysis of the K-12 schools market for serious games in the US, that some of the primary challenges that companies face in the successful distribution of serious games in schools are creating or obtaining a distribution network and achieving consumer acceptance as "the long, painful process of personally establishing a distribution network is a major reason serious games are so slow to appear in schools" (2011, 89). Policy intervenes in these objectives by defining how curricula can incorporate exploratory, open-ended, or 'fun' instruction associated with games. The barriers for incorporating games in education are therefore often the ways in which national curricula and models for schooling are excluding games by adapting the understanding of teaching and learning to standardised testing and curricula. It can be argued that these policy-defined processes significantly narrow the scope for game-based learning (Mayo 2011, Scanlon & Buckingham 2004).

In this chapter we shall focus on policy as an aspect of how serious games become included in or excluded from educational practice. We shall suggest that researching policy becomes one way of acquiring knowledge about how serious games can become a part of teaching and learning in schools. Our data originate from the Serious Games on a Global Market Place project, for which a number of actors identified as policy makers were interviewed in order to study national frameworks for education and learning.

In this chapter our focus is mainly on data which have been produced at various levels of national and local government through interviews with actors involved in policy making. We approach the issue of policy through four case studies of educational policy in Denmark, Portugal, Vietnam, and the UK. These case studies are interpreted through a variety of primarily anthropological theories that understand policy as complex articulations of cultural and social ideas of the educated person (Levinson & Holland 1996, Shore & Wright 1997). We shall argue that the identification of policy actors and of policy as a phenomenon that affects actors and practices is in itself a methodological issue that is not easily defined or resolved.

2. POLICY IN THE INFORMATION SOCIETY

The study of policy involves the identification of policy as an actor in social and cultural processes relating to, for instance, education. Policies may be understood as instruments for promoting efficiency and governance, but also, inspired by anthropological perspectives, as cultural agents that reveal the processes and ideologies of societies themselves. As argued by Shore and Wright (1997), policies are not 'neutral' instruments for promoting efficiency or governance; they can themselves become methods for studying how cultural and social norms are codified by nation states and how they infiltrate institutions and everyday life with ideologies and power. In the anthropology of policy, as it is conceptualised by Shore and Wright, it is therefore essential to understand policy as a cultural agent and a political technology that exists at several levels of society and is constituted through processes of struggle and contestation.

Policies can be understood as key features of modern power and governance that exist at the level of documents, institutional practices, and interactions between citizens and government officials. However, policy also has a legitimising role, for instance in forging social identities such as the active (European) citizen, the self-managing individual, or the competent child

(Shore & Wright 1997, Gitz-Johansen 2004). In this sense it can be argued that the frontiers of policy are expanding to incorporate the individual's sense of self and identity as well as the large-scale creation of social identities. The objectives of these policy processes may be both nation-building in a competitive global economy where education is understood to be a central asset, and the regulation of individuals to conform to these objectives.

The role of policy in creating subjects that are digitally literate and can respond to the demands of the knowledge society is specifically significant in the study of serious games, as games may or may not be conceptualised as contributing to the strategies of school reform and innovation associated with ICT in education policies of nation states. As mentioned above, serious games are emergent technologies that are often not mentioned explicitly in curricula and other kinds of policy initiatives related to formal education (though there are significant exceptions to this rule). Serious games are in this sense peripheral to educational policy, where priority is generally given to the large-scale implementation of ICTs in schools. The conceptualisation of the learner as a serious gamer may therefore to some extent collide with the idea of the competent, self-regulated learner who is a central actor in the emergent globalised information society. These conceptualisations of the learner are central classificatory strategies that are found in national and global policies for education.

In our serious games study we have understood the integration of serious games in formal education as an aspect of digital literacy initiatives in policy, i.e. as connected to state-endorsed strategies for the implementation of ICTs in schools. This is arguably a methodological choice; we could have conceptualised games differently, and provided different results. However, the comparative nature of our studies in ICT policies in education and the focus on games as a part of these policies has contributed to an understanding of how, why, and where serious games are connected to the idea of the emergent information society, and what this means for the market for serious games in formal education.

3. POLICY AND THE MARKET FOR SERIOUS GAMES

Understanding policy in relation to the market for serious games involves identifying and studying the idea of the market itself. In the wake of the emergent information and knowledge society the conceptualisation of the market has changed to afford new connections between public and private actors and between nation states and global actors in education. These changes have opened educational markets to new actors such as private companies who focus on producing learning materials for children and young people inside and outside schools.

One of the most significant changes in the market for education in the past decades has been the connection of information and knowledge to the economic growth and development of nation states (Kearns 2002). Anderson-Levitt (2003) suggests that neoliberal movements on the market for education have introduced new agendas such as "choice" and "marketization" for schooling, and that the consequent decentralisation and deskilling of teachers has put more pressure on, for example, parents as educators. Shore and Wright similarly observe that market metaphors have infiltrated government itself, and that government has been transformed into a form of enterprise that is organised through pseudo-markets such as schools and hospitals. The idea of education and learning as a market therefore underscores the convergence of economic objectives with social change and innovation, which places private enterprise and innovation through research in a central position.

With regard to the marketization of education, Scanlon and Buckingham (2004) argue that parental investment in education has increased as the growing competition for educational advantage has affected the role of parents and children as educational consumers. This has boosted opportunities for the sale of educational material and hardware to children for home learning, but also the market for learning material that links content directly to the curriculum, to school work, and to assessment (Scanlon & Buckingham, 2004). However, research generally indicates that the market shares shrink as the child ages (Mayo 2011), and that serious game developers must identify alternative markets for games – or comply more strategically with curriculum aims and tests – if they want to succeed.

In the Serious Games Project we have focused on the role of serious games on a global educational market, in order to understand how they can be developed and designed to compete on that market. Our research has involved strategic cooperation between universities and companies with the intention of identifying innovative markets for serious games produced by private companies rather than, for instance, publishing houses. We have understood the market for serious games in terms of these new public/private partnerships in education, as a central aim of the project has been to explore the development of innovative relationships between these actors (in this case game developers and universities). In this sense we have contributed to an understanding of how the marketization of education affects serious games developers who are not part of the established market for educational material, which is currently represented by publishing houses, among others.

In the Serious Games Project we have initially understood the global market for education as consisting of a number of nation states that represent individual educational cultures which can be compared with respect to curricula, educational traditions, teacher education etc. This approach has been based on our initial idea that educational markets are to a large extent characterised by national values and traditions and that it will consequently be vital to acquire specific knowledge about educational contexts in different countries. In the course of analysing data our perspective has gradually shifted from a focus on the nation state as a primary site for the study of educational policy to the incorporation of multiple sites of policy making within and across nation states (inspired by for instance Marcus 1995; see below). This shift has been brought on by the process of following specific games (www.mingoville.dk, www.globalconflicts.eu) into local sites for teaching and learning, specifically schools and classrooms in Denmark, Finland, Norway, and the UK, where we have conducted fieldwork. These field studies have pointed to policy as an actor in a variety of social and cultural contexts relating to education. In other countries such as Singapore, Hong Kong, and Vietnam we have – due to budget and time restraints – followed policy exclusively as a part of state and municipal governance through interviews with policy makers and the study of relevant documents, such as curriculum aims. In these contexts the process of research has revealed that policy makers at state and municipal levels themselves often understand policy as a complex phenomenon that consists of a variety of connections between (perceived) instruments of efficiency such as documents, assessment strategies, and cultures of practice.

Our research into the educational policy of nation states has also uncovered policy as a phenomenon that constitutes both systems of governance and cultural meaning within nation states (and to some extent serves to define them), and models of practice that are distributed and shared globally between nation states. One of the reasons for the existence of these distributed models of education (and strategies for the implementation of ICTs in schools) are the pressures of efficiency and standardisation that arise from transnational bodies such as the OECD – as well as the general focus on innovative solutions for successful education in the information society. Another reason, as argued by Anderson-Levitt (2003), is the origin of school systems in colonial processes where education systems have often been modelled on western concepts of education, originating mostly in the US and UK. The idea that education may be understood both as divergent systems of schooling created by modern nation states and as converging systems of schooling that can be identified as global models for education is at the centre of both Anderson-Levitt's argument and our research. As proposed by Anderson-Levitt, it can be argued that what we can identify as convergent or divergent in global schooling is dependent on the level of abstraction that we choose for our analysis, and that fieldwork and the local knowledge acquired by anthropologists significantly challenges the idea of a global culture of schooling. In fact, Anderson-Levitt, inspired by Spindler and Spindler (1990), suggests that what may stand out as consensual global models of schooling can be approached as evidence of cultural dialogues across nations, an approach that will stress the idea of the complexity in schooling and of conflicts within and between nations as part of a struggle with meanings. This view would comply with our observations of diverging and converging models for disseminating ICT in education, models that are articulated in and represented by policy.

4. RESEARCHING POLICY: THE QUESTION OF METHODOLOGY

As mentioned above the methodological reflections involved in our research situate serious games in global/local relationships with policy making in the information society. In our approach to studying policy in these global/local contexts, we have been inspired by anthropological theory, for example Shore and Wright's policy of anthropology discussed above (1997) and George Marcus' multi-sited ethnography (1995). The significance of Marcus' discussion of world culture theory and his challenge to the concept and methodology of single-sited ethnography is that it provides the basis for understanding fieldwork not only as the single-sited ethnographies that inform classical studies in anthropology but as mobile ethnographies that "examine the circulation of cultural meanings, objects, and identities in diffuse time-space" (1995, 96). These multi-sited ethnographies are characterised by breaking out from single-sited studies to "empirically following the thread of cultural process itself", i.e. into following moving actors and concepts in postmodern societies. In his multi-sited ethnography Marcus consequently identifies a number of ways of following cultural processes (actors and concepts) empirically, including following the people, following the thing, and following the metaphor. Following the metaphor – as an example – relates to tracing modes of thought and the circulation of signs and symbols, an approach that we feel is at the heart of researching policy, as policy can be understood as systems of representation that often involve metaphorical thinking. Following people and things on the global market may be equally significant to research in policy, as researching global markets for education involve empirically following things (for instance 'commodities' such as computers, serious games) as well as people (for instance pupils, teachers, government officials). In our fieldwork and interviews with government officials we have repeatedly encountered the idea that policy involving ICT in education can be articulated as systems of thought that are inspired by metaphorical representations such as rings in water, phases, and levels etc. In addition to this, policy makers point to the connections between the systems of thought implied by policy and the people who interpret and implement policy. In the following four country case studies we shall identify the ways in which we have followed policy and the ways in which policy makers understand policy as systems of thought that implicate people and things, and how these can be followed. We shall suggest that these analyses provide examples of networks of dissemination that may help serious games developers to understand how, where, when, and through whom they can disseminate their learning products.

5. MAKING CONNECTIONS – GLOBAL AND LOCAL ISSUES IN RESEARCHING THE POLICY OF ICT IN EDUCATION

The four countries studied below represent four examples of how policy is articulated as a complexity of connections between relevant actors in education and systems of thought that underpin objectives of implementation and innovation in schools through the dissemination of ICTs. The four countries represent a sample of the country studies that we have carried out in the Serious Games Project in the period 2009-2011. The country cases studied in the project have been chosen for their perceived significance for the companies and the serious games involved in the study. In Portugal, for instance, we followed the game-based platform Mingoville into schools as a major state-endorsed policy initiative involved distributing laptops to children in which Mingoville was a recommended learning material for teaching and learning English. In the UK we have focused on how an articulated policy of using serious games for innovative teaching and learning in schools may facilitate dissemination and use of the serious game Global Conflicts. Other parameters for the choice of country cases have been their cultural and geographical positions in the world (for instance Nordic countries, European countries, Asian countries), their perceived high (or low) status in educational standards (Finland), or in their innovative use of ICT in education (Singapore). The four case studies chosen for this chapter represent different cultural and geographical positions in the world as well as diverging and converging approaches to the dissemination of ICT in education.

Though the study of policy from an anthropological perspective entails following the modes of thought and the connections made by policy makers between actors, institutions, and government bodies, we also wish to frame our analysis in terms of hypothesised convergent and divergent tendencies on the global market for education. Anderson-Levitt (2003) argues, as mentioned above, that neoliberal approaches to schooling have entailed a marketization of education, a marketization which results in the fact that decentralisation of, for instance, management and school choice is a powerful force in many countries. On the other hand, the standardisation of testing and curricula as well as the control of teachers and a focus on content-centred instruction is a visible effect of new conceptualisations of schooling that may be understood as contradictory to the focus on decentralisation. Finally, many countries understand student-centred instruction and learner-centred pedagogy as a central issue in schooling for the 21st century, an idea that is often connected with digital media and with new approaches to teaching and learning associated with these media.

With regard to the implementation of ICT in education Kearns (2002) argues, on the basis of a multi-country analysis of trends in policy for ICT in education, that many countries go through the same foundational phases in their policy for ICT in education. According to Kearns these are:

Phase one: rolling out computers into schools and colleges with some professional development of teachers and development of online content.

Phase two: mainstreaming and integrating the role of ICT into education in a more strategic way with more concern for objectives, and with linkages forged to overall education strategies (Kearns 2002, ii).

Finally, according to Kearns, a number of countries stand on the threshold of a third phase of development, which might be more radical with respect to the way teaching and learning is conceptualised as part of the information society. An aspect of the third phase in policies for ICT in education may be an explicit articulation of innovation as part of the strategies for using ICT in schools. It may be expected that, since Kearns' study, a number of countries have moved into the third phase of ICT policy in education, though it should be remembered that not all countries move at the same pace or have the same priorities. The following (brief) case studies will discuss to what extent the educational policies of the chosen nation states articulate connections between phases in the development of ICT policies for education, and how this complies with their ideas of the general trends in education, including the cultural production of the educated person (Levinson 1997). The case studies are therefore essentially narratives of the connections articulated by policy makers between large-scale trends in education and the role of serious games.

5.1 DENMARK

During the past decade there has been an increasing emphasis in Denmark on getting computers into schools, on educating teachers, and on producing digital and online learning material for specifically elementary schools. This focus on ICT in education corresponds roughly to the foundational phases described by Kearns (2002) above. A possible third phase of ICT in education policy has been initiated in the past year; for example, more emphasis has been put on the integration of digital learning material in schools.

In the past decade there has been a number of large-scale government initiated projects in Denmark that have focused on implementing the use of ICT in schools. These are: ICT and Media in elementary school (ITMF 2002-04), ICT in elementary school (ITIF 2004-07), and, as mentioned above, a new initiative is on its way this year which aims to support a fuller integration of ICT in schools and classrooms. In the ITIF project the focus has been on distributing computers specifically to 3rd form pupils (age approx. 9) and on developing digital learning materials for elementary schools. A significant element in the policy of ICT for education is a principle of government funding, which means that the government has supported a number of private companies and publishing houses financially in their work with developing digital learning material, some of which are learning games. In our project, we have followed one of these learning materials: the game-based platform Mingoville.

In Denmark we have interviewed two policy makers, a government official at ministerial level who has been involved in curriculum development for elementary school, and an official at municipal level who has been involved in distributing and assessing a number of government funded digital learning materials for elementary schools. The relationship between these two levels of policy making is that the municipality studied has recently initiated a large-scale free distribution of the digital learning material which has been funded by the ministry as part of the ITIF project (2004-07). In this sense we have followed a chain of policy that has incorporated a strategy for the distribution of ICT into elementary school, the development of digital learning material to enhance this strategy, and a municipal strategy to support the use of these digital learning materials in schools in a specific local area. This chain of policy has involved the research-based development of the game-based learning material Mingoville, and has in fact contributed to the marketing of this material. It has been the explicit policy of the present Danish government to establish relationships between the public and private sector, and the ITIF project (as well as our research) has been a part of these strategies, which has opened up new markets for private investments in and developments of learning material, including the game-based material Mingoville.

The policy maker we interviewed at ministerial level is both an active teacher and a government official. Her perspective on policy is therefore based on a double view, the view of governance and the view of practice. This double view gives us an insight into how policy is understood and how it acts at several levels of the education system.

At the ministerial level the articulation of what policy is and what its objectives are is primarily associated with documents such as curricular and cross-curricular aims. In 1993 the Ministry of Education introduced a more standardised and aims-oriented curriculum than had previously been the case for elementary schooling. However, though these curriculum aims are increasingly used by the Ministry of Education in, for instance, assessments for national tests, they are still only guidelines, which means that it is up to the individual municipalities, schools, and teachers to interpret them. This is a principle of decentralisation that is pervasive in the Danish school system at the same time as policies at the ministerial level increasingly focus on standardised national testing and government initiated assessments of pupils' skills.

The Ministry of Education official focuses part of her account for the ministry's ICT in education policy on the relationship between two documents, the national curriculum aims (Fælles Mål 2009) and the aims for the integration of ICT in schools (It- og mediekompetencer i folkeskolen 2010). The latter document focuses specifically on how to use ICT in schools, including web 2.0 media, and is a development of aims for the use of ICT found in the 2009 curriculum document. She also mentions the role of the ITIF project as significant in getting ICT into schools.

In her role as a teacher she points to a number of issues at the practical level that may work against the intentions of policy. With regard to digital learning material for instance, there is the problem of schools having to buy the material (such as Mingoville) rather than getting it for free from the ministry. The digital learning materials that have been supported financially by the government cannot be given to schools for free because of market restrictions. This should be seen in the context of the general pressure on school budgets. To a large extent, she argues, schools are using free material found on the internet for teaching, rather than investing in licenses. The implementation and free flow of policy intentions into practice may therefore be hindered by these restrictions, as well as a number of other practical issues including how teachers are motivated to use new materials for teaching.

Our interview at the municipal level focused on a policy for ICT education in a municipality situated in the eastern part of the country. The policy maker we interviewed has been a teacher for many years as well as a consultant in ICT for learning. Her view is also the double view of governance and practice; however, at the time of the interview she was deeply engaged in the municipal project of getting teachers to use the ITIF materials.

At the municipal level studied the ICT in education policy is understood in the context of decentralisation. Decentralisation is in this case understood as a challenge, as it generates the need for an initiation of policy strategies that will enable relevant ICT use to spread automatically through the relevant bodies to actors, specifically teachers and learners. In the studied municipal context policy has, as mentioned above, focused on the dissemination of digital learning materials through a municipal investment in free user licenses for schools. Nine digital learning materials have been chosen that cover the subjects of Danish, science, maths, and art. These learning materials have all been funded by the Ministry of Education in connection with the ITIF project.

The interviewee presented us with a number of metaphorical representations of the current dissemination process of the ICT policy for education. One of these is the idea that policy (and thereby innovative activity and initiatives) can be spread like 'ripples in water', i.e. concentrically from a centre which is represented by municipal initiatives and governance. The basis for this conceptualisation of the policy of dissemination is among other things the reality of decentralisation, which requires that policy can become a self-directed force that is initiated and takes strength from one conceptual centre. In the case presented this centre is the municipal strategy for the dissemination of the learning materials described above. The centre of the concentric circles is therefore a number of introductory activities that introduce teachers to the learning materials and the possible use of these materials in classrooms. Introductory activities may involve short courses or guidance by municipal advisors in the classroom (or the computer lab). Introductory activities are thus identified as central to the role of the municipal actors in disseminating materials, whereas other actors such as school leaders and (head)teachers are supposed to carry out the dissemination activities at the next levels of the dissemination process. An additional metaphor for the dissemination process used by the interviewee was therefore the idea of 'joints', i.e. that teachers and pupils are the most distant joints of the policy implementation, the end points of the process, and the actors at which dissemination of learning materials and their proper use is directed. It is the municipal aim of reaching these central actors that is the real challenge of the dissemination process in the context of decentralisation.

5.2 PORTUGAL

In Portugal during the last couple of years there been a massive effort to integrate ICT in schools; recently there has been a specific focus on primary schools. During 2009 a number of initiatives for the development of pupils' ICT competences were launched at the government level. The national effort has primarily focused on getting computers and interactive boards into schools, i.e. what corresponds to Kearns' first phase of ICT development as described above (2002).

Portugal has consequently invested a lot of money in hardware. First of all, the government has focused on distributing computers to pupils at a primary school level. Prior to this, secondary schools had been equipped with computers, several hundred per school, depending on the size of the school. Training of the teachers is going to follow as a second phase of ICT integration. The education ministry plans to provide three levels of training. The first concerns ICT skills; the second is on the educational use of ICT; and the third level includes training on how to use computers in education especially for the teachers who are going to train other teachers.

In Portugal we interviewed a government official at ministerial level who has been involved in the national ICT policy for primary school and acts as a representative of the English teacher association, which has been developing the curriculum for English as a foreign language in primary education. Locally, we have interviewed a teacher who also functions as a consultant for local government with the task of selecting and developing learning materials for the teachers and pupils in the municipality.

In the interviews we often encountered the idea that ICT is a reform actor in education, i.e. that ICT has the ability to facilitate the transition of nations and learners into 21st-century schooling and that "things will change in very little time". This expression is employed as a conclusion to the descriptions of various efforts such as distributing computers to the youngest pupils, and getting computers and interactive whiteboards into schools. The expression must be interpreted as a conviction that ICT development will proceed quickly once schools are provided with computers.

Portugal's current ICT policy for primary schools is characterised by an ICT strategy with a main focus on pupils. ICT as an artefact becomes the central actor in this strategy, which is called the Magellan project – inspired by the 16th-century Portuguese explorer. The Magellan project is a joint venture with Microsoft to accelerate technology adoption in Portuguese schools. The aim of this project is to distribute Intel Classmate laptops to all pupils in primary school.

The purpose of providing children with laptops is to enhance children's ICT and English language competences. Thus the aim of the Magellan initiative is to prepare new generations for learning in the information society. Laptops are specifically given to the children themselves and not to schools. The idea is that if the computers belong to the schools the pupils cannot bring them home. By giving the computers to the children, the responsibility for the computers rests on the children and their parents; the effort must therefore be understood in relation to the parents who will consequently have the opportunity to use the computers with their children. Making the computers the children's property will allow them to use their computers in their spare time and thus develop their ICT and language competencies.

However, the intention is also that the computers should be used primarily in and for school. When the children receive the computers they have learning content and links relevant to schooling installed. On each computer, for instance, there is a desktop link to the online English language learning platform Mingoville that we are following.

As mentioned above, the Magellan project is a comprehensive effort on the part of the government for integrating the use of ICT in schools; however, through our fieldwork we discovered that there had been several problems with it locally at different schools, as the infrastructure is generally not upgraded. For example, some schools do not have enough chargers for the laptops, which essentially means that the daily use of the computers at the school is dependent on whether the computers are charged when the students arrive. Also, internet connections and Wi-Fi may not be reliable. This means that pupils may not be able to use their computers to go online.

In relation to the teacher level of ICT policy, the ministry has constructed an online repository of digital resources to be implemented in a so-called school portal and all schools are being equipped with interactive white-boards, which the teachers are obliged to use.

The ICT strategy at the pupil and teacher levels is a centralised approach. The centralised approach is based on a weak infrastructure; but in some schools, we saw examples of a decentralised approach. In the local area we visited, the teachers and pupils had received USB-keys with subject content from the local school authority. This teaching material was called "manual digital". Locally, the municipality is developing their own ICT strategies with a focus on the teachers. The USB-keys contain learning materials which are partially developed and selected by a group of local consultants and teachers who also continuously update the content. This means that the interactive whiteboards distributed to schools are actually integrated in teaching and learning. The municipal strategy of directing policy at teachers thus seems, based on our fieldwork (2009), to be successful compared to the government strategy of targeting children's use of ICT.

In Portugal it is the local school authority that is responsible for imple-menting the policy set by the ministry. The policy of implementation is decentralised in the sense that it is the individual schools who decide how ICTs are used. The state thus provides the actors with ICT artefacts with the idea that the artefacts will be used by the actors: "The teachers are going to be obliged to use computers in one way or another, and this means than they might be using more games than before […] and the teachers are able to access thousands of digital learning resources, these resources might be more widely used in schools". In Portuguese education, learning games are considered a means to, for example, motivation recall and memorisation. In this sense games are understood as specifically relevant for primary school education and for training specific skills.

5.3 VIETNAM

Education generally has a high priority in Vietnam. Because of this, there are high expectations in the country regarding the contribution of ICT to education and society, and the government has developed Master plans for

ICT in education and for ICT and Human Resource Development (Prime Minister 2009). A gap between policy and practice exists in Vietnam, as in other countries; for instance, a study of five teacher education institutes in Vietnam found that, in principle, there is "a high appreciation of ICT for education, but in practice, ICT is mainly used to replace existing teaching practice" (Peeraer, Tran, & Tran 2009, 1).

In Vietnam, we interviewed two policy makers: a Deputy Director General of the Department of Primary Education in the Ministry of Education and Training (MOET), who offered a general view on initiatives in the educational system from a Ministerial perspective; and a researcher and Deputy Director General of the Vietnam Institute of Educational Sciences (VNIES), a research institute under the Ministry, who had been particularly involved in a reform of the teaching of foreign languages that is currently being implemented.

The Vietnamese government has made an effort to establish broadband internet connections to all schools, which should be implemented by the end of 2010, and to establish computer labs in all secondary schools. This corresponds to the initial phase of ICT implementation described by Kearns (2002) above.

In our interview, the Ministry representative stated that "For lower secondary and upper secondary, each school is provided with one computer lab for students. But for primary, it is not implemented yet. Some primary schools may have a computer lab, based on the contribution of the parents or of some company in the locality, but they are not provided by the Ministry."

Computer and internet access contribute to the competitive advantage of the primary schools that are in a position to provide them for their pupils without Ministry funding. However, because computers are not available in all primary schools, ICT is not fully integrated in the primary school curriculum:

"In the national curriculum, ICT is just mentioned as an elective subject, called Informatics, just to familiarise the children with the use of computers, like learning how to prepare a Word document, or how to paint using the Paint programme, or just to be familiar with using a computer. That's all. So they are modest objectives." (Interview, Ministry representative).

Private expenditure on education in Vietnam is estimated to account for the same amount as the state expenditure on education (London 2011, 86). This is visible in that the establishment of computer labs in primary schools is partly dependent on private funding, and it corresponds with Scalon & Buckingham's notion (2004) mentioned earlier that parental investment in education is growing.

Curriculum development in Vietnam is structured as a very centralised process. There is one set of textbooks in each discipline at each grade, which is taught in every school in the country. The curriculum framework of each discipline and grade are developed in detail by VNIES and approved by the Ministry. On the basis of these curricula, the national Education Publishing House develops corresponding textbooks and teachers' guides, which are also approved by the Ministry and serve as nationwide teaching materials. This requires a long process of central decisions, development, approvals, and implementation to establish new teaching methods and create new teaching materials.

During the last ten years, the Education Law of Vietnam has emphasised that the goal of education is to implement "an active learning approach" and to produce "active and creative students" (Nguyen 2009); in the new English curriculum, it is stated that "the child will be the centre of the learning process" (interview, VNIES). The aim of this policy is to change the traditional teaching method, which generally consists of the teacher lecturing, and the students listening carefully and taking notes. However, even compared to the long process of changing the curriculum and developing new teaching materials based on active learning approaches, changing the actual practice of teachers will take a very long time. It will require a considerable effort from the Ministry, including further education of teachers.

Another challenge is related to the teaching of foreign languages, which is at present being reformed. Currently, students start their first foreign language, usually English, in grade 6, but in the future they will be introduced to a foreign language in grade 3. This change demands a new curriculum as well as new teaching methods, partly because of the younger age of the children, and partly because of a general change towards focusing on what communicative competences the students need.

The reform of foreign language teaching underpins a demand for more and better-qualified English teachers. The number of new teachers needed is currently not met by the educational institutions, and the general level of the existing English teachers also needs to be raised.

The general policy of the Ministry is to encourage the use of ICT, but there are some reservations:

"The Ministry always has the policy to encourage the teachers to use ICT in their teaching. However, […] the use of ICT must serve the central purpose of the curriculum or the subject. […] So they give the warning that ICT should not be overused." (Interview, MOET)

This scepticism is not limited to government; there have been debates in public newspapers as well as in the Ministry concerning the growth of the internet and online games cafes, which caused worries that students would spend all their time playing games or surfing the internet, and would not be able to attend their classes properly. As a result of these debates, in 2010 authorities decided to prohibit internet cafes within a 200-metre radius of schools, and to shut down the internet connections of internet cafes at night time.

However, the view on games is far from being solely critical, and the Ministry encourages teachers to use games as part of their teaching:

"For example, we also encourage teachers to use games to teach maths, or to let the children just play with Maths." (Interview, MOET)

In collaboration with a Vietnamese technology corporation, FPT, The Ministry has launched a nationwide educational online game contest in maths. The game is organised into different levels of competitions where the goal is to be the best student at solving maths problems. The competitions are for students to participate in individually, in their spare time, whenever it suits them. The game is not a translation of an existing game, but was developed by Vietnamese programmers, and consists of 15 or more rounds of maths problems that have to be solved in a set time. Winners are issued with a certificate and the students with the most points are mentioned on the game's website. A similar game has been developed for English teaching. The English game follows the same format as the maths competition, but was developed by a different Vietnamese partner, a Cable Television company.

6. UNITED KINGDOM

The development and integration of ICT in the UK is progressing unevenly across and within schools and technologies, which means that some schools have prioritised certain technologies such as interactive whiteboards, whereas other schools have put more emphasis on innovative uses of technology

(Condie et al. 2007). Even though there have been several projects initiated on game-based learning related to ICT policies in the UK, the following analyses show how the English and Scottish initiatives differ markedly in terms of promoting centralised versus decentralised approaches to such initiatives. However, contrary to the situation in the other countries included in this analysis, game-based learning is a formulated part of education policy in the UK – though the approaches to GBL differ within local (English and Scottish) governments.

6.1 ENGLAND

Within the past decade, there have been numerous research projects conducted in England that have explored the learning potential of games as a part of the national ICT policies. Following the TEEM report on the educational use of games (MacFarlane, Sparrow, & Heald 2003), the government funded technology agency BECTA (1998-2011) and the government co-funded research and development organisation NESTA FutureLab (2001-) have conducted a number of literature reviews, surveys on the use of games in schools, and intervention projects on how to teach with commercial computer games (i.e. Sandford, Facer, Ulicsak, & Rudd 2006). Recently, the change of government in 2010 has led to the closing down of BECTA, which has resulted in decreased government funding opportunities for research projects on game-based learning.

In order to identify different policy aspects of the game-based learning initiatives in England, we conducted interviews with two representatives from BECTA, before it was closed down, and a senior researcher from NESTA FutureLab. We also interviewed an ICT consultant working at a county council, who has helped to develop game-based learning within primary and secondary schools for a number of years; this provided a more local perspective on the use of games in schools.

The representatives from BECTA and NESTA FutureLab pointed to the fact that game-based learning – whether it is based around serious games, commercial computer games, and/or students designing games – remains a relatively marginal activity within the English school system compared to other ways of using ICT. In spite of the relatively large amount of game-based learning initiatives funded or co-funded by the state government, the different projects can mostly be described as rather decentralised or isolated attempts in the sense that they have had limited implications for the national curriculum. As one of the BECTA representatives argued, the educational value of game-based learning as a more effective way of teaching and learning has not yet been scientifically proven. Because of this lack of evidence for the support of game-based learning in relation to the curriculum, there have not been sufficient incentives for putting game-based teaching higher up on the national educational agenda. Another reason for the marginal status of games in the English educational system is that they are difficult to "fit into" the curriculum. This is especially true in relation to secondary and upper secondary schools, where there is more pressure on schools, teachers, and students to achieve good grades. Thus, both representatives from BECTA and FutureLab emphasised that teachers need to ensure that students are able to meet curriculum objectives when teaching with games. At the same time, both the informants from BECTA and FutureLab predicted that the market for serious games would grow in the years to come, with particular regard to games that address primary schooling, as they overlap with the consumer space outside formal schooling. Finally, there was general agreement that the recent change of government would lead to increasing decentralisation in terms of using games, as decisions on whether or not to invest in games for educational purposes would be left up to each individual school.

We also interviewed an ICT consultant who worked at a county council to support game-based learning on a local scale. In contrast to the BECTA and NESTA FutureLab representatives, he was a former school teacher and was able to view game-based teaching both from an insider's perspective (as a teacher) and from an outsider's perspective (as a consultant). His overall perspective on the use of games was that it was "slowly creeping in" to the English school system as more and more teachers were becoming familiar with the learning potential of games. He emphasised the same barriers to using games in schools as were mentioned above: technical issues, lack of time in the schedule, problems with fitting games into the curriculum, and convincing teachers and parents of the educational value of games. At the same time, he also stressed the role of the individual teacher in being able to understand game mechanisms and to evaluate the learning potential of a particular game. This dual difficulty for teachers of understanding games and matching them with curricular objectives was confirmed in our qualitative study on how teachers enacted the Global Conflicts series at an English school (cf. Hanghøj & Brund, in this book). Still, the ICT consultant we spoke to was quite optimistic about the future possibilities for using games in the English schools, mainly because teachers are increasingly required to be able to design their own lessons and learning activities, which may also include the use of games.

6.2 SCOTLAND

As is the case in England, the Scottish government has also supported game-based learning for a number of years as a part of its national ICT policy. In 2006, Learning & Teaching Scotland, a non-departmental public body funded by the Scottish government, established The Consolarium, which works with teachers in order to explore and share how the appropriate use of computer games can have a positive impact on teaching and learning. Since its inception, The Consolarium has initiated numerous projects, some of which involve the use of commercial games such as Guitar Hero and Dr. Kawashima's Brain Training in the classroom (cf. Robertson & Miller 2010).

However, in comparison to the English initiatives, The Consolarium marks a wholly different policy approach to game-based learning. First of all, the initiative can be described as far more centralised as it forms an integrated part of the state government and is closely linked up with the development and implementation of the new Scottish Curriculum for Excellence. This has not been the case with the English examples mentioned above, where BECTA mostly commissioned research projects that had limited integration in the national curriculum. Secondly, The Consolarium also differs from the initiatives in England as its projects are based more on a bottom-up structure, with more involvement from the participating teachers. According to the manager of The Consolarium, this strategy of identifying interested teachers and working closely together with them in relation to their own aims forms a large part of the explanation of why game-based learning is slowly becoming a mainstream activity within the Scottish educational system. The strategy is further described in the quotation below:

"So our work has been from the ground up working with teachers; sharing ideas at local authority conferences; going to schools and working with parents and teachers; sharing on national websites; speaking at conferences; and gathering up a momentum of influence."

Because of this bottom-up strategy, the informant from The Consolarium suggests that game-based learning has become "an established and accepted aspect of the wider landscape of teaching and learning in Scottish schools."

A second difference in the Scottish policy relates to the material used in game-based learning. The Consolarium has chosen to focus its initiatives on commercial games such as Guitar Hero and Neverwinter Nights and game design projects, rather than using serious games. This strategic focus on commercial games and game design is also backed at the national level by the Scottish Curriculum for Excellence, which explicitly states that young people should learn how to become creative media users through the process of designing and understanding games (Robertson & Howells 2008).

A third explanation for the increasing use of game-based learning in Scotland can be attributed to the game pedagogy employed in many of The Consularium's projects. Several of these are based upon attempts to use games to create "contextual hubs", i.e. using games as a stimulus or basis for creating game-related learning environments. This means that the overall aims are not necessarily to teach game design or games as such, but rather to introduce Guitar Hero, Neverwinter Nights, or other types of games as a means for creating environments that students can explore in relation to a number of different curricular aims.

The point here is that games are not seen as ends in themselves, but rather as a means to facilitate other learning activities. This also means that games are seen less as exotic phenomena imposed from the outside, but as learning resources that can be closely integrated with teachers' everyday demands.

In summary, the interviews indicate how both the English and Scottish governments have been quite willing to fund projects that have aimed to explore and develop the educational use of computer games as a part of their national ICT policies. However, the examples discussed above also suggest that the deployment of two different strategies has produced widely different results.

7. IMPLICATIONS OF THE POLICY STUDY

In this chapter we have argued that policy can be understood as an aspect of how nation states articulate and legitimise governance. We have also argued that policy can be found in diverse linguistic articulations and actions (for instance, documents and interpretations of documents) that cut across government bodies and institutions. Finally, we have pointed to the possible connections – and tensions – between the policies of ICT in education and the implementation of serious games in formal education.

The country cases analysed above indicate that the status of games in policy for education is relatively marginal in a number of countries, where the primary focus is on creating competent learners for the 21st century by integrating ICT policies in schools. According to our studies, large scale ICT and education policy strategies thus dominate the field of education policy at both municipal and ministerial levels. These large scale initiatives revolve around the global issues of standardisation and decentralisation trends in education, of pupil and teacher roles, and new public-private relationships, as suggested by Anderson-Levitt (2003). In addition to this, policy makers generally characterise policy as an instrument for promoting efficiency and reform and for forging societies and individuals that will be competitive on the global market.

Serious games and game-based learning are involved in the policy processes of integrating the use of technology in schools. However, it is not obvious from our analysis exactly how the role of game-based learning is understood in the individual countries as part of the broader educational aims suggested by policy. This may be a problem associated with methodology, as our study has hypothesised and looked for connections between game-based learning and larger national perspectives on education – specifically those that involve digital media. A closer look at local education initiatives might thus have revealed a stronger interest in and implementation of game-based learning. On the other hand, it is evident from studies such as those made by anthropologists and sociologists of world cultures of schooling that national and transnational trends in education (including the discourses of New Public Management) are becoming increasingly significant for how nation states conceptualise and formulate their educational policies. Serious games and game-based learning are not, according to our studies, strongly connected to these global trends in education.

As our studies indicate, ICTs, but not necessarily digital games, are understood by policy makers as actors that facilitate and accelerate the transition of nations and learners into the emergent information society. In this context ICT competences – and often also language competences (in English) – become indicators of basic 21st-century literacy skills. Game-based learning may be associated with these skills, as for instance in Scotland where media creativity and the design of games are understood as central competences for new generations of learners. However, the view of games may also be more sceptical – as in England, where the focus on efficiency and standardised curricular aims may exclude games from formal education. The perspective on serious games may also be ambivalent, as was the case in Vietnam, where gaming is seen both as a disruptive activity to be banned (as part of what goes on in internet cafes) and as an activity that can enhance competition and engagement in the learning of central skills such as maths and English. Throughout these analyses, we find the idea that serious games have a significant role to play in primary education for basic skills that can be trained through memorisation and recall. This view of games is in many ways different from an exploratory view in which games are understood as agents for creativity and student-centred production of knowledge (as in Scotland). Thus the concept of serious games and the definitions of their purpose in education shift as much as the concepts of education and learning themselves.

The ways in which serious games and game-based learning are involved in broader educational trends and policies are thus both complex and inconclusive. The connections between game-based learning and local, national, and global policies may be difficult to identify because serious games is not a mainstream discourse in education, but also because connections are difficult to make when phenomena are not easily compared (Strathern & Edwards 2000, Marcus 1995). However, serious games and game-based learning are articulated as phenomena that have a role in the education of 21st-century learners, though the character and strength of these articulations vary within the national policies for education in which they are embedded.

The case of the UK seems to indicate that game-based learning may be an emergent discourse in policy that has not yet gained hold in the other countries analysed, possibly because their cultures of education are not yet open for the kind of explorative and innovative approach to teaching and learning that game-based learning may represent. However, an evolutionary perspective on the role of game based learning – corresponding to Kearns' three phases of ICT implementation – is not really deducible from the data analysed, as games are connected to multiple aspects of education, among them the idea that game-based learning supports training and memorisation in basic subjects. Our focus on policy has therefore uncovered the idea of serious games and game-based learning in formal education as multiply defined and multiply situated in policy initiatives for 21st-century schooling.

8. IMPLICATIONS FOR SERIOUS GAMES DEVELOPERS

Merrilea J. Mayo proposes that game developers often have to make distribution paths for their products themselves in order to penetrate the school market. The challenge faced by serious games developers is therefore to persuade central actors in education such as teachers, pupils, school leaders, and parents that games are materials and contexts for learning that can contribute to producing competent 21st-century learners.

In this chapter we have argued that game developers may connect their market strategies to an understanding of how policy works as a cultural agent in defining and producing the educated person (and nation). We do not know what the relationship is between policy and practice; however, we are proposing that game designers join forces with researchers in order to understand how policy works to define the market for game-based learning. The practice of following policy as an actor on the educational market may, we propose, help us to understand the multiple local and global paths for the distribution, marketisation, and production of games that can be successful in schools and for learning.

REFERENCES

Anderson-Levitt, K., ed. 2003. *Local meanings, global schooling: anthropology and world culture theory*. New York: Palgrave McMillan.

Condie, R., B. Munro, S. Seagraves, & S. Kenneson. 2007. *The Impact of ICT in schools – a landscape review*. BECTA.

Egenfeldt-Nielsen, S. 2004. "Practical barriers in using educational computer games." *On the Hori* 12(1).

Egenfeldt-Nielsen, S. 2010. "The Challenges to Diffusion of Educational Computer Games." In Meyer, B. (ed.) *Proceedings, European Conference on Game-Based Learning*. Academic Publishing Limited.

Gitz-Johansen, T. 2004. "The incompetent child: Representations of Ethnic Minority Children." In *Beyond the competent child*, edited by H. Brembeck, B. Johansson, & J. Kampmann. Exploring contemporary childhoods in the Nordic Welfare States. Roskilde University Press.

Hanghøj, T. & B. Meyer. 2010. "How to study something that does not (yet) exist." In Meyer, B. (ed.) *Proceedings, 4th European Conference in Games Based Learning*. Academic Publishing Limited: Reading.

Kearns, P. 2002. "Towards the Connected Learning Society. An International Overview of Trends in Policy for Information and Communication Technology in Education." Available at http://www.dest.gov.au/NR/rdonlyres/5526D69E-132A-454D-B916-FBA0B8E86811/912/towards_the_connected.pdf, accessed on November 9, 2011.

Levinson, B. A. & D. Holland. 1996. *The cultural production of the educated person: an introduction*. State University of NY Press.

London, J. D. 2011. "Historical Welfare Regimes and Education in Vietnam." In *Education in Vietnam*, edited by J. D. London. Singapore: Institute of Southeast Asian Studies. 57-103.

MacFarlane, A., A. Sparrowhawk, & Y. Heald. 2003. "Report on the educational use of games." TEEM.

Marcus, G. E. 1995. "Ethnography in/of the World System: The Emergence of Multi-Sited Ethnography." *Annual Review of Anthropology* 24, 95-117.

Mayo, M. J. 2011. "Bringing Game-Based Learning to Scale: The Business Challenges of Serious Games." *International Journal of Learning and Media* 2: 2-3.

MOET (Ministry of Education and Training, Vietnam). 2004. "Current Situation of Vietnamese Education." In *Vietnam Education and Training Directory*, 3rd ed. Hanoi: Education Publishing House. 16-26. Available at http://en.moet.gov.vn/?page=6.1&view=3451, accessed on April 11, 2011.

Nguyen, H. C., ed. 2009. *Vietnam Education in the early years of the 21st century.* Hanoi: Vietnam Education Publishing House.

Peeraer, J., N. M. T. Tran, & T. T. H. Tran. 2009. *Policy Analysis Integration of ICT in Higher Education in Vietnam.* Paper presented at the International Workshop on Policies for Teachers and Educational Leaders in Innovative Education Process. Available at http://daotaoquocte.edu.vn/eng/include/coe/conference2009/25.Anh.pdf, accessed on February 25, 2011.

Prime Minister, Vietnam. 2009. *Decision: Approval of the master plan on Information Technology (IT) Human Resource Development (HRD) through 2015 and Orientation towards 2020*, 698/QĐ-TTg C.F.R. (2009).

Robertson, J. & C. Howells. 2008. "Computer game design: Opportunities for successful learning." *Computers & Education* 50(2): 559-578.

Robertson, D. & D. J. Miller. 2010. "Using a games console in the primary classroom: Effects of 'Brain Training' programme on computation and self-esteem." *British Journal of Educational Technology* 41(2): 242-255.

Sandford, R., K. Facer, M. Ulicsak, & T. Rudd. 2006. *Teaching With Games. Final Report.* London: Nesta FutureLab.

Scanlon, M. & D. Buckingham. 2004 "Home learning and the educational marketplace." *Oxford review of education* 30: 2.

Shore, C. & S. Wright. 1997. "Introduction. Policy: A new field of anthropology." In *Anthropology of Policy*, edited by C. Shore & S. Wright. New York: Routledge.

Spindler, G. D. & L. Spindler. 1990. *The American cultural dialogue and its transmission.* Falmer Press. London, New York, Philadelphia

Strathern, M. & J. Edwards. 2000. "Including our own." In *Cultures of relatedness: new approaches to the study of kinship*, edited by J. Cambridge: Cambridge University Press.

2 C. MULTI-SITED ANALYSIS OF GAME-BASED LEARNING

Bente Meyer

1. INTRODUCTION

Though comparative education studies often situate education in cultural contexts (Broadfoot 1999, Alexander 2001, Osborn et al. 2003), it has been argued that experiences and discussions within ethnography have not been sufficiently included in comparative education studies (Hoffman 1999, Sørensen 2008). This is particularly relevant when comparative education studies focus on the social and cultural impacts of globalisation as these require a re-conceptualisation of the spaces within and across which education becomes possible.

In this chapter I shall discuss how comparative methodologies can be conceptualised and used in educational contexts where online learning games are involved and where times and spaces for engagement in learning and in education are shifting and multiply situated. I shall argue that multi-sited ethnography (Marcus 1995, 1998, Falzon 2009) is a relevant methodological framework for studying the shifting settings in which educational games become embedded and make sense. In multi-sited ethnography the borders and contours of what can be studied comparatively are challenged, as it focuses on distributed knowledge systems and on emergent objects of study in global settings. Marcus' revision of concepts of site and field within anthropology thus reminds us that comparative studies, including studies in comparative education, is a changing discipline that is affected by transnational and crosscultural movements in education, learning, and pedagogy (Marcus 1995, 2009, Carney 2009).

2. LEARNING ENGLISH WITH MINGOVILLE

In 2009 a group of researchers (of which I was one) was preparing some fieldwork in Portugal; a learning platform for English as a foreign language (www.mingoville.com) was the main object of study. The purpose of the research was to conduct a comparative study based on the idea that serious games (i.e. online game-based learning material) had a global potential in language education and that ethnographical studies could enhance an understanding of how online game-based teaching and learning could be developed for and through educational practice in different localities. One of the main propositions of this research was that educational markets are characterised to a large extent by national values and traditions; and hence, that it was vital to acquire specific knowledge about these educational contexts in different countries. In a sense this comparative study therefore rested on the understanding that global significance and market development was researchable "within" and "between" national contexts of education, and that these could be compared through an assemblage and juxtaposition of field analyses.

However, as work progressed questions about the spatial organisation and delineation of the fieldwork repeatedly presented itself to members of the research group. The problem of spatial delineation was related to the specific challenges involved in studying the platform in question. Mingoville.com is a learning platform for teaching children English as a foreign language and is currently marketed as "The World's Most Comprehensive Online English Lessons for Kids – for free!" Mingoville is accessible online and can therefore in principle be used anywhere at any time.

Mingoville is a phenomenon that is not easily captured in terms of what it is and what it does in educational contexts (Hansbøl 2009). First of all, as an educational material Mingoville is constantly developed and therefore altered, to suit the needs of learners, parents, and teachers. These developments usually consist of minor technical adjustments or added tasks such as seasonal competitions. However, in 2009 a major development called Mingoville Virtual World was added to the platform to increase user interest and activity. The addition of the new Virtual World zone significantly altered teachers' and pupils' entry to the platform between our first and second fieldwork studies, making the process of comparison of the 'bounded' platform Mingoville more complex.

Secondly, Mingoville is involved in different kinds of cultural flows in the sense that it addresses a global market for teaching and learning English. The global orientation of the platform is, for instance, presented in the claim that Mingoville is the world's most comprehensive collection of online material for English, as well as in the statement, on the home page, that Mingoville currently has over one million users worldwide. On the home page the user will find testimonials from users from all over the world, explaining how and why they are using Mingoville.

Originally, Mingoville was developed to suit the needs of the Danish curriculum for teaching English in primary school; however, the designers of the platform also assumed that teaching English in primary education would be similar in a number of countries across the world, i.e. that it would be based on basic vocabulary areas such as numbers and letters, animals, the family, and the body. According to comparative studies in world systems of schooling (Anderson-Levitt 2003), elementary curricula are relatively similar around the world, and pre- and primary school education are often the educational levels targeted by commercial designers of digital learning material (Buckingham 2007). In this sense the creation of online teaching and learning material for primary schools addresses both the ideals of nation-building involved in elementary schooling (Anderson-Levitt 2003) and the global aspects of schooling associated with online material and especially with English as a lingua franca.

Mingoville is, I am proposing, a new type of learning material that cannot be fully understood and studied within the borders of a national education culture. As an online learning material for teaching and learning English, Mingoville does not confine itself to specific national cultural traditions of education, though it does try to address the realities of linguistic differences between national cultures. Our multi-sited analysis will add to the study of how Mingoville moves – and is moved – on and by a global market.

3. COMPARATIVE STUDIES IN ETHNOGRAPHY – A MULTI-SITED APPROACH

Studying a moving phenomenon like Mingoville requires a research design that can grasp both the contours and qualities of Mingoville as a game-based learning platform, including the varieties of settings in which it may have a significance for teaching and learning English. Ethnographical studies provide the main framework for the study in question, as ethnography contributes to a situated understanding of how games may interact with language education (Meyer & Holm Sørensen 2009, de Castell & Jenson 2003). In the context of comparative studies, ethnography is understood as a methodology that can both study and constitute sites that provide the basis for a comparative study. However, as I shall argue below, education studies that involve ethnographical perspectives are not inherently comparative, but can become so if several sites are involved and these sites can be connected to understand the phenomenon in question (Sørensen 2008, Marcus 1995).

Briefly put, ethnography can be understood as a methodological intervention in which the researcher is deeply involved in local knowledge, i.e. in participating in, observing, and mapping specific social and cultural practices and how these emerge and unfold over time and in space – or across times and spaces (Gupta & Ferguson 1997, Olwig & Hastrup 1997). In 'classical' ethnography the field has often been conceptualised as a single site in which participation over time has involved a holistic understanding of knowledge, i.e. the idea that cultural meanings are relatively stable and can be studied within single sites over time. However, as spaces and objects of research have been affected and transformed by the mobilities and displacements of late modern societies, such as diaspora and globalisation, ethnographical studies have similarly dispersed and decentralised into multiple sites in which fields are "substantially continuous but spatially non-contiguous" (Falzon 2009). This is what Marcus, as mentioned above, has coined as 'multi-sited ethnography' (1995, 1998, 2009), i.e. an ethnographical approach that focuses on chains, networks, and juxtapositions of locations rather than single-site studies.

Marcus' multi-sited ethnography addresses the comparative dimensions of ethnography, i.e. it does as Marcus says "represent a revival of comparative study in anthropology" (1995, 102). However, as a comparative strategy, multi-sited ethnography is not, as has been mentioned, a controlled comparison, juxtaposing stable, clearly bounded phenomena, but a process in which connections are made through movement and discovery among sites. This construction of movements among sites is contained in and epitomised by Marcus' tracking strategies, i.e. what he calls following the people, following the thing, following the metaphor, following the plot, story, or allegory, following the life or biography, and following the conflict. As knowledge and cultural production in postmodern societies is distributed across sites, tracking becomes a strategy for the ethnographer to produce knowledge, a strategy that draws up a social and cultural landscape in which objects of study are not clearly bounded and distinctive. Comparison, from this perspective, is not unfocused or unwilling to carve out links and relationships, rather it is comparison that incorporates movement (of people, metaphors, and 'things' as well as the ethnographer) into the construction and identification of comparability.

For game-based language learning – the focus of this paper – movement and distributed knowledge is significant on a number of levels. First of all ethnographical knowledge is significant for the study of educational gaming because the question of how games are involved in learning must be answered from within the spaces and experiences that generate 'game-based learning', i.e. through local knowledge. In addition to this, game-based learning can be understood as something that is produced and distributed across time and space, specifically as games and game-based learning material has become a commodity that is circulated through, for instance, the internet. According to Scanlon and Buckingham (2004) and Buckingham (2007), computers have been central in the commercialisation of home tutoring in the UK, for example, and edutainment and game-like material have been significant commodities – that are 'child-centred' – in this market strategy. This means that learning through games is not restricted to formal education and to the distribution of learning material within institutionalised settings. In addition to this, English as a world language – the learning 'content' of the platform studied – is an important commodity in a globalised world, as English has not only historically been a language of privilege, but remains a privileged skill in global economies, and in many countries across the world English is seen as key educational investment (Graddol 2006, Philipson 1992). Following Mingoville therefore involves, among other things, tracking the significance of English as a world language in 'global' settings for education.

4. WHAT MOVES MINGOVILLE? – TRACKING MINGOVILLE IN THE WORLD

Marcus defines 'following the thing' as a tracking strategy that essentially focuses on following manifestly material objects through chains of commodity framed by capitalist societies. The point of these studies is mainly to allow the idea of the system to emerge ethnographically by following paths of distribution and circulation in these societies (Marcus 1995, Appadurai 1986). In addition to this, Marcus suggests, when the thing traced is situated within realms of discourse, ethnographical research may also involve tracing signs, symbols, and metaphors significant to and associated with the research 'object'. The idea of the thing in Marcus' theory may therefore be understood as existing between the manifest and the metaphorical, i.e. as something that is conceptualised both as a commodity with identifiable borders and material qualities and as something that is constituted in discourse and where boundaries may be less certain. Though both of these conceptualisations of Mingoville may be understood to be discursively constructed as social manifestations of the platform, they are also different positions that influence how Mingoville can be followed, understood, and researched.

In relation to our research on Mingoville, both the metaphorical and the material aspects of the platform as a 'thing' to be followed were significant. During the project we met regularly with the company that had designed Mingoville in order to understand how their market strategy and their business model for Mingoville supported the circulation of the platform in different cultural contexts and how this would be significant for research. These meetings helped us to understand how the company primarily understood the platform as a commodity to be marketed and sold, but also how the adaptation and assimilation of the platform to different learning contexts was central to the socio-material constitution of the platform and its educational values.

For the company, Mingoville's marketability was dependent on both its stability as a learning platform that engages children in learning English through the 'fun' of gaming, and its ability to adapt to different cultural contexts of education. From the perspective of the company, understanding Mingoville as a global actor would therefore entail both seeing it as something that distinguished itself from other products on the market – for instance commercial games or game-based platforms that did not have an educational purpose – and as something that might address and be a part of different (national) contexts for learning English around the world. In the latter capacity, Mingoville would often be seen as something that was both culturally bounded and unbounded, and could engage children across borders as well as work in different spaces and across spaces that might be relevant for education and learning. The division between Mingoville School and Mingoville Virtual World was in this context essentially a way of addressing the different spatial organisations of learning of which Mingoville could become a part, including homes, libraries, and after school centres as well as classrooms.

Following Mingoville from an ethnographical perspective therefore first of all required a research design that could describe and encompass the cultural adaptations and global flows of the platform without disregarding the significance of (national) borders that were defined in our own research, and in the platform itself, as significant for the production and distribution of serious games. This to some extent entailed a delineation of potential markets and fields in which and across which Mingoville might have a role in teaching and learning English.

5. FIRST STUDY: FIELDWORK IN PORTUGAL

Following the methodological framework of our project we focused the first part of our fieldwork on a Portuguese locality, as the Portuguese Ministry of Education had been involved in a distribution of the Mingoville platform into Portuguese classrooms through a recent policy initiative. This distribution of Mingoville was an important marketing strategy for the company, as the material would be included in a major national strategy for distributing computers to children in primary education in Portugal. Mingoville would thus potentially become a part of the nation-building involved in including computers in primary education as the pupils' tool for learning.

The context for this centralised national distribution of Mingoville was a high-profile education technology plan called the Magellan Initiative, in which 500,000 Intel Classmate PCs had been distributed to primary school children throughout the country during the school year 2008-09. Mingoville was pre-installed on these computers as a desktop link together with other educational games, creating the possibility of learning activities with Mingoville in Portuguese schools, as well as related research activities that might identify the emergence of Mingoville as a participant in local educational practices.

Though the Magellan project had supported the presence and distribution of Mingoville as something that could be accessed for free through the laptop computers, the emergence of Mingoville as an actual participant in practice was however not immediately viable in the specific locality and time we had chosen for our research. This became obvious to us through communications with teachers and our local translator prior to our fieldwork and to some extent required a re-conceptualisation of our research design, which will be described below.

In the local context of our field study the (non)emergence of Mingoville as a player in the specific school context we studied (English teaching in the fourth grade) was dependent on a number of conditions for educational ICT-based practice embedded in the local practice at that time. These conditions contradicted the idea that distributing the Classmate PCs to pupils for enhanced elementary learning would in itself support and qualify 21st-century learning strategies. For example, the school infrastructure did not generally support the use of the laptop computers as wireless internet was not accessible to pupils in the classroom. In addition to this, there were not enough plugs to recharge the computers, which could only run on battery for a very limited time. Finally, for various reasons teachers preferred to or were left to use the interactive whiteboards installed in the classrooms and the teaching material produced by the local municipal authorities rather than engaging in online learning platforms like Mingoville. One reason for this teaching practice was that the computer lab in which learners would have been able to access online material was usually used for teaching pupils ICT at the time when English was taught. This meant that computers with internet access was generally inaccessible to English teachers and their pupils during scheduled lessons.

Though Mingoville was significantly linked to the national Portuguese initiative for developing primary education through the distribution of Classmate computers to Portuguese children, the manifestation of Mingoville as something that could emerge as a learning material for teaching English in primary school was not visible in the school we visited due to local conditions for teaching and learning online, as described above. Thus following Mingoville into the Portuguese setting identified aspects of the material, i.e. its dependence on online accessibility, that might prevent its circulation within and across spaces into which it had been distributed. Accessibility is, needless to say, a basic condition for online teaching and learning, as is local infrastructure and support.

In order to study the use and educational significance of Mingoville in the Portuguese locality we therefore had to set up a practice with the platform during our visit, i.e. some English lessons were moved from the classroom to the computer lab in order to make Mingoville accessible to and playable for teachers and learners. This intervention became necessary as a consequence of the non-emergence of Mingoville in English teaching in our field during our week of fieldwork (and beyond), which in turn was an aspect of the multiple local conditions for teaching and learning in which Mingoville was involved.

6. SECOND STUDY: FIELDWORK IN FINLAND

As mentioned above, multi-sited ethnography conceptualises comparison as a process that is ongoing and that relies on establishing connections between sites that may be "worlds apart" (Marcus 1995). The discovery of these connections relies on an understanding and analysis of how things, metaphors, people etc. move and are partially present in different locations or in distributed networks. In our research we sought to understand both how Mingoville could become (or not become) a part of practice within the frameworks of national curricula and policies and how connections between different spaces or locations in which Mingoville had been materially or metaphorically present could be established. What we have delineated are therefore movements in which Mingoville took part and which have been ethnographically discovered by following paths of distribution and circulation in specific localities.

In our second fieldwork study we travelled to Finland to follow Mingoville into a school in which a specific teacher had been using Mingoville periodically in the 3rd, 6th, and 5th form for English. The framework for this fieldwork was to some extent, as was the case in our first fieldwork, the national conditions for game-based learning in English as a foreign language. However, in our second fieldwork study the national distribution of the platform in elementary education was not an issue for our research, as no similar political strategies that included Mingoville had been initiated in Finland. In the Finnish school we visited the teacher had been introduced to the platform through her own search for relevant online learning material for English – thus Mingoville was moved by the practice and into the practice of this teacher.

Unlike our research in Portugal, in Finland we had been able to localise an educational context in which Mingoville had a role and a presence, and which could be studied through ethnographical presence. Following Mingoville in this case meant studying the movements of the platform primarily at the micro level of teaching English in an elementary school without the added political framework of building national strategies for the use of ICTs in primary education.

Our research began at a point when the teacher had been using the platform for a couple of months, and had integrated this use into the 5th and 6th form teaching mentioned above. Prior to our fieldwork we had a number of Skype conversations with the teacher in order to understand how she was using Mingoville in her teaching and how she was planning to use Mingoville during our stay. Our fieldwork in Finland consisted of observations of classes with and without Mingoville as well as conducting interviews with pupils, teachers, and the school leader (who happened to be the English teacher).

Though our fieldwork in Finland involved many of the same methodological approaches as had been employed in Portugal, i.e. ethnographic approaches, the focus and scope of our studies in Finland were of a different nature. In the Finnish locality Mingoville was present as a significant and visible part of learning English in school (and outside school, for home learning), though aspects of how Mingoville was included in practice were to some extent dependent on the set-ups necessitated by research (see below). The significance of the differences between these two field studies was therefore primarily a possible comparison or connection of the ways in which Mingoville could become a part of English teaching, as well as an experience of how these insights could be understood by research.

Following Mingoville into the Finnish locality first of all made us aware of the variety of ways in which it could be included in and interact with other aspects of English teaching, such as teaching in class and learning at home. As in Portugal, Mingoville was primarily made accessible in school from the Finnish school's computer lab, to which pupils of the 5th and 6th form were sent to do specific tasks chosen by the teacher. In the Finnish locality, using Mingoville in the computer lab was part of a pedagogical framework used by the teacher, which entailed that the class would be divided into groups of 5-8 pupils who would then take turns to participate alternately in classroom teaching and learning with Mingoville. The purposes of this division were, among other things, to target and support pupils with different intellectual or subject competences, to vary the pace and approaches to learning, and to support different kinds of learning styles.

Within the arrangements set up by the teacher in the Finnish locality Mingoville had a role as a learning platform that (as understood by the teacher) might support a number of skills and purposes related to teaching and learning English in that specific locality. Though accessibility to Mingoville was a recurrent issue affecting how, when, and by whom Mingoville could be used, it was – during the week of our fieldwork – nevertheless integrated into practice in a variety of ways. Accessibility issues were generally associated with 'technical problems' affecting how Mingoville could become playable – and accessible for learning – by individual pupils. Thus 'technical problems' influenced the length and quality of individual pupils' interaction with the platform: at the same moment in time some pupils would have no problems with access and others would have to continuously log on to tasks without gaining access. However, there was no single explanation for these connection failures. Still, the issue of accessibility was a central concern for the Finnish teacher, a concern that could possibly affect her use of Mingoville in the future.

To conclude, our studies in the Finnish locality gave us the opportunity to study practice ethnographically in different kinds of teaching and learning arrangements in which Mingoville was a part. In this context experimental interventions were generally not necessary as existing practices provided us with knowledge of and experience with locally embedded possible uses of the Mingoville platform, i.e. specific tasks in the platform. However, this is not to suggest that our presence as researchers did not affect practice; for instance, the teacher involved told us that she might not have insisted that pupils should repeatedly log on when platform tasks did not work – for whatever technical reasons – and that she might – had we not been there – have rearranged some sessions to not include Mingoville.

Finally it can be argued that the Finnish study identified a number of ways in which Mingoville could be understood to move with and within English teaching, specifically as an element in distinguishing and differentiating between different learners, skills, and motivations. As mentioned above, Mingoville consists of a number of game-based activities that, specifically in the Mingoville School zone, are well suited to support language teaching that organises learning into 15- or 20-minute slots to support learner skills, learning styles, and motivation. In the Finnish school a number of teachers claimed that this spatio-temporal organisation of learning was integral to their teaching style and that the organisation of teaching that we had observed had been acquired by most of them at university, during teacher education. Thus, Mingoville seemed to fit into a local teaching style that became the reason for its relative success in this locality.

7. CONCLUSIONS – COMPARISON FROM AN ETHNOGRAPHICAL PERSPECTIVE

In this chapter I have argued that multi-sited ethnography can contribute to the field of comparative education studies as it can provide situated knowledge about teaching and learning, and identify and trace movements and flows in and between cultural settings for education – from a global perspective. In addition to this, I have argued that multi-sited ethnography conceptualises and traces comparative perspectives of education studies in ways that may challenge comparative studies that understand comparison as something that can emerge within predefined frameworks of similarities and differences.

Studying the flows and movements within and across sites – which may be understood as more or less bounded – can be specifically relevant when the focus of comparative study is a game-based learning platform like Mingoville that is distributed and marketed for learning, or edutainment, worldwide. Education and learning is thus an expanding concept including (specifically since the spread of the internet) not only a variety of materials and temporal organisations of access and presence, but a spatial reorganisation that is a consequence of both the globalisation of education systems and assessment, of the integration of digital media in education and learning, and of the marketisation of educational media, materials, and methodology. Comparative education studies should be able to study these flows and movements in which online education takes part.

Although multi-sited ethnography is to some extent ideally suited to studies of global systems of distribution or movement, this approach does have its problems as a methodology, as suggested by Marcus himself (Marcus 2009). First of all, it has been suggested that multi-sited ethnography is a weakly defined concept that does not really break with conventions within classical ethnography, specifically single-site ethnographies (Falzon 2009, Hage 2005, Candea 2007). On the other hand there is a concern within ethnography that multi-sited ethnography adds to the dilution of ethnographical practice and rhetoric as these have been critiqued during the 80s and 90s following the "writing culture" and "writing against culture" turns within anthropology, in which Marcus himself was involved (Clifford & Marcus 1986, Abu-Lughod 1991). The effects of these revisions of ethnographical practice are, as voiced by this critique, that analysis of multiple sites compromises the ethnographer's ability to do thick description (Geertz 1973) and that multi-sited ethnography therefore remains incomplete (Horst 2009, Marcus 2009). Though these critiques of multi-sited ethnography may very well be relevant, especially from a single-sited perspective, it must be remembered that the point of multi-sited ethnography is exactly that people, metaphors, and things are only partially present in single sites and that a number of phenomena (if not all phenomena) cannot be understood by focusing on single sites. Although the ethnographer does spread her energy, attention, and allotted time between sites in multi-sited ethnography, these distributions of interest reflect the networks in which actors and commodities participate and make sense. As noted by Horst (2009), depth and multi-sitedness can therefore be well combined.

Focusing on Mingoville as a platform that is embedded in the movement and flows of the global market and education settings highlights the fact that the educational design of online game-based material for teaching and learning can benefit from understanding design as both a stable and as an adaptable phenomenon. This involves understanding both the similarities in education systems across the world, for instance the principles and strategies within and across elementary educations worldwide, as well as the local differences and conditions for online learning. It is the potential connections and links between these sites of teaching and learning that constitute a multi-sited ethnography of game-based learning.

REFERENCES

Abu-Lughod, L. 1991. "Writing against culture." In *Recapturing anthropology: Working in the Present*, edited by R. G. Fox. Santa Fe: School of American Research Press.

Alexander, R. J. 2001. *Culture and Pedagogy*. Malden: Blackwell.

Anderson-Levitt, K., ed. 2003. *Local meanings, global schooling: anthropology and world culture theory*. New York: Palgrave Macmillan.

Appadurai, A., ed. 1986. *The Social Life of Things: Commodities in Cultural Perspective*. Cambridge University Press.

Broadfoot, P. 1999. "Not So Much a Context, More a Way of Life? Comparative Education in the 1990s." In *Learning from comparing*, edited by R. J. Alexander et al. New directions in comparative educational research, vol. 1. Oxford: Symposium Books.

Buckingham, D. 2007. *Beyond technology. Children's learning in the age of digital culture*. Cambridge: Polity Press.

Candea, M. 2007. "Arbitrary locations: in defence of the bounded field-site." *Journal of the Royal Anthropological Institute* 13(1). 167-184.

Carney, S. 2009. "Negotiating Policy in an Age of Globalization: Exploring Educational 'Policyscapes' in Denmark, Nepal, and China." *Comparative Education Review* 53(1). 63-88.

Clifford, J. & G. E. Marcus, eds.. 1986. *Writing culture. The poetics and Politics of Ethnography*. Berkeley: University of California Press.

de Castell, S. & J. Jenson. 2003. "Serious Play." *Journal of Curriculum Studies* 35(6). 649-665.

Falzon, M. A. 2009. *Multi-sited ethnography. Theory, Praxis and Locality in Contemporary Research*. Surrey: Ashgate Publishing.

Geertz, C. 1973. *The interpretation of cultures*. New York: Basic Books.

Graddol, D. 2006. *English next*. British Council. Available at http://www.britishcouncil.org/learning-research-english-next.pdf, accessed on November 9, 2011.

Gupta, A. & J. Ferguson. 1997. *Anthropological Locations. Boundaries and Grounds of a Field Science*. Berkeley: University of California Press.

Hage, G. 2005. "A not so multi-sited ethnography of a not so imagined community." *Anthropological Theory* 5(4).463-75.

Hansbøl, M. 2009. "Getting In-formed. Researching Circulations and Establishments of a So-called Serious Game." Unpublished paper, the Danish School of Education.

Hoffman, D. M. 1999. "Culture and Comparative Education: Toward Decentering and Recentering the Discourse." *Comparative Education Review* 43(4): 464-488.

Horst, C. 2009. "Expanding Sites: The Question of 'Depth' Explored." In *Multisited Ethnography. Theory, Practice and Locality in Contemporary Research*, edited by M. A. Falzon. Surrey: Ashgate Publishing.

Marcus, G. E. 1995. "Ethnography in/of the World System: The Emergence of Multi-Sited Ethnography." *Annual Review of Anthropology* 24. 95-117.

Marcus G. E. 1998. *Ethnography through thick & thin*. Princeton University Press.

Marcus, G. E. 2009. "Multi-sited ethnography: Notes and queries." In *Multisited Ethnography. Theory, Practice and Locality in Contemporary Research*, edited by M. A. Falzon. Surrey: Ashgate Publishing.

Meyer, B. & B. Holm Sørensen. 2009. "Serious games – research and design for game based language learning in a global perspective." In Pivec, M. (ed.) *Proceedings, 3rd European Conference on Game-Based Learning*. Reading: Academic Publishing Limited.

Olwig, K. F. & K. Hastrup. 1997. *Siting Culture. The shifting anthropological object*. New York: Routledge.

Osborn, M. et al., eds. 2003. *A world of difference?: comparing learners across Europe*. Buckingham: Open University Press.

Philipson, R. 1992. *Linguistic Imperialism*. Oxford: Oxford University Press.

Scanlon, M. & D. Buckingham. 2004. "Home learning and the educational marketplace." *Oxford review of education* 30(2). 287-303.

Sørensen, E. 2008. "Multi-Sited Comparison of 'Doing Regulation.'" *Comparative Sociology* 7: 311-337.

3. EDUCATIONAL DESIGN

EDUCATIONAL DESIGN FOR SERIOUS GAMES

Birgitte Holm Sørensen

1. INTRODUCTION

This article focuses on the construction of a concept for the educational design of serious games. On the basis of the project Serious Games on a Global Market Place, a concept is proposed for an educational design incorporating theories of didactics and of learning including formal and informal learning, games, play, communication and multimodality, and various pedagogical approaches. This concept furthermore includes reflection on children and children positioned as pupils, as well as the role of the teacher in relation to serious games. The model has been refined throughout the project's three-year duration (Sørensen & Meyer 2010, Sørensen 2009a, 2009b).

Using games in lessons provides a challenge to educational design on two levels. The first challenge concerns the construction of the game itself, which raises a number of questions; the second concerns the usage of the game in actual lessons within various subject-specific and cross-curricular contexts, where issues of educational design become relevant regarding, for example, planning, and teacher and pupil participation.

2. INTRODUCTION TO A CONCEPT OF AN EDUCATIONAL DESIGN FOR SERIOUS GAMES

This section presents a concept of an educational design for the development of serious games. The theoretical foundation for this educational design has its roots in constructivist, experience-oriented, and social learning theories including formal and informal learning, didactic categories such as teacher and pupil positions, relations and roles, forms of learning, theories about games, play, communication and multimodality, and various pedagogical schools of thought including Computer Supported Collaborative Learning focusing on collaborative processes and the function of language therein, and project pedagogy focusing on problem definition, production, and independent working processes.

In relation to teaching, the concept of design can be defined as the plan or the model for which activities or artefacts should be included in which teaching and learning contexts, and when. Educational design can be defined as the process by which the framework, planning, organisation, and arena for teaching and learning activities are constructed against a background of theory and in relation to practice within a given context. Educational design can be carried out in relation to teaching and learning within contexts (face2face, virtual and mixed mode), and in relation to the development of ICT-based learning products (learning materials, learning platforms etc.). Furthermore, educational design can function as a tool for analysing teaching and learning within contexts and ICT-based learning products in terms of what constitutes the underlying assumptions or educational designs of those situations and products. The concept is illustrated in the model below, which is then discussed in further detail.

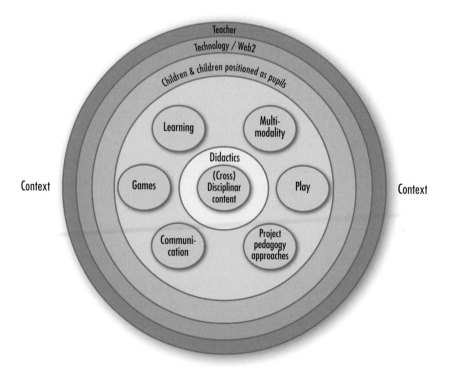

Figure 1: *Didactics*

3. SUBJECT-SPECIFIC/CROSS-CURRICULAR CONTENT

According to Gee, computer games teach players to participate in a semiotic domain, which is to say an area or a set of activities where people think, act, and appraise in a particular manner (Gee 2007b), and where one or more semiotic modalities, such as verbal language, pictures, symbols, sounds, graphs, artefacts etc., are employed in communication and action. When children play *SimCity*, for example, the semiotic domain is city planning, design of buildings, roads etc., and city governance; within this domain they employ a number of modalities which appeal to reflection and assessment.

Figure 2: *SimCity*

In a school context, the various topics broached in lessons can be considered as semiotic domains. When designing serious games, the aim is to ensure that the game's semiotic domain corresponds with semiotic curricular content. This applies to the project-affiliated learning game Global Conflict: Palestine, where the semiotic domain is the conflict in the Middle East, corresponding to curricular content within the subjects of History and Social Studies.

Figure 3: *Global Conflict: Palestine*

The subject-specific or cross-curricular content is the overriding focal point for the educational design. There is considerable variation in terms of the subject area(s) in question. In Mingoville, a game-based learning platform for English as a foreign language, the focus is entirely on language, while Global Conflict, a serious game with themes of democracy, human rights, globalisation, terrorism, climate, and poverty, can be used in cross-curricular contexts as well as in individual subjects such as History, English, and Social Studies. The subject-related topics or semiotic domains act as a starting point for determining which activities the class can work with. Within a global market perspective, it is also of significance whether or not the subject-related content is connected to curricular content with relevance to national curricula in a number of countries, particularly those countries with marketing interests. The subject-related content and the didactic approach to this content are fundamental to the game's ongoing educational design.

4. DIDACTICS

The development of digital teaching and learning products has focused attention on didactics. The concept is primarily based upon more recent Germano-Scandinavian didactic approaches operating with a broad definition of didactics as theories about and reflection upon objectives, goals, content, planning, preparation, and assessment of teaching and learning (Hopman & Riguarts 1995, Hiim & Hippe 1997, Schnack 2000).

As such, didactics within the Germano-Scandinavian tradition encompasses three didactic levels: the practice level, the preparation level, and the level of theoretical reflection (Dale 1989, Dale 2000). The three levels are mutually dependent and interact with one another; together they are regarded as a whole.

When applying the concept of didactics to serious games, the focus is upon the didactics built into the game's design and upon the didactic application in the context in which the game is expected to be used. There are both formal and informal educational contexts: Mingoville, for example, the game-based learning platform for teaching foreign languages, can be used at school in English lessons and by pupils in their free time who want to learn English. Didactic thinking regarding these two contexts considers, among other things, that a formal context includes a teacher's role and an informal context does not. Mingoville's didactic design uses these two contexts; the platform can be divided into Mingoville School, which has been designed specifically for a school context, and Mingoville Virtual World, which has been designed so that the children are able to work by themselves, with no teacher involvement. Nevertheless, both sections of the learning platform can be used in both contexts.

Bolter applies the concept of remediation (Bolter 1999) to describe the process whereby digital media absorb older media, which are then refashioned in various ways and take on new forms of manifestation. On the didactic plane, this entails a re-didactification, that is to say a didactic rethink, redevelopment, and/or enhancement of the didactic categories and their inter-relationships.

There is great potential present in both digitalisation and the internet for changes to educations that may result in radical transformations of learning and teaching processes. For decades, the printed book has constituted the central learning artefact; however, during the course of the last ten years, this position has increasingly been contested by digitalised teaching and learning artefacts. This development has highlighted the importance of the learning artefact with regard to its implied learning potential, the didactic thinking behind it, how it can be used in lessons, and what it means for the pupil's learning. The book as learning artefact rests upon a long tradition of development and research which has been influenced by shifting trends in pedagogical and didactic approaches and by developments within learning theory.

The game as learning artefact poses a considerable challenge to the field of didactics, as games constitute a break with a whole string of ways of teaching and learning within the context of the school. The extensive interest in serious games within the context of the school can first and foremost be attributed to an assumption that games contain certain potentials for learning – an assumption founded on children's great interest in computer games outside the school.

5. LEARNING

In conjunction with educational design for serious games, it is relevant to consider learning as a process which operates within a social field and in a context influenced by interrelationships and reciprocity. Learning is understood as both a result and a process. When coupled with digital media, learning is understood as an individual and social process of construction and negotiation within a context. Change and difference are central concepts in definitions of learning. This is especially true when learning is considered as the result of learning processes which are understood as producing a difference or change in relation to something previously learnt (Hermansen 2001, Illeris 2006). Learning can also be understood as what Knud Illeris has described as a cognitive, psychodynamic, and social, societal process (Illeris 1999).

Social learning processes can be understood both as a prerequisite for and contributor to individual learning processes, and as a situation in which the individual contributes to the construction of the shared learning process. Social learning processes thereby become a reflection of what a group of individuals learn within a community and can as such be regarded as learning which is shared by a group, although without this shared learning necessarily also finding expression in the individual learning of each group member. Etienne Wenger's theory of learning within communities of practice constitutes a central element in the social approach to learning (Wenger 1998).

A central element of children and young people's learning is the distinction between formal and informal learning. In a recent literature review article, Julian Selfton-Green pinpointed various definitions of formal and informal learning, definitions which are frequently connected to the contexts within which learning is situated (Selfton-Green 2006). As such it might be suggested that it is not so much a case of formal and informal learning as of formal and informal learning contexts.

The concepts of formal and informal learning are applied here based on the approach of a play culture. For children and young people, formal learning is tied to the school/educational institution and learning is an *objective* of the activities which take place. Informal learning is characterised by a primary setting away from schools/educational institutions and is a *means* to acquire ability and knowledge applicable to activities such as, for example, playing computer games, chatting online, and writing a blog. In order to be able to play, the children have to learn something (Jessen 2001). Learning thereby becomes a prerequisite for and an integral part of children and young people's play activities; for instance, when Danish children and young people participate in online games for which the operative language is English, they have to master new terms and phrases. In such cases, the children themselves are proactive and take the initiative with regard to learning something new, and learning English becomes a means in order to be able to play the game. During formal English lessons in school, various activities are organised where the objective is that the pupils learn English. When these two approaches are combined into learning strategies, they prove to be effective ways of learning (Sørensen, Audon, & Levinsen 2010).

In children's leisure culture, for example when playing computer games, a number of different informal forms of learning can be observed which function in different contexts and are occasionally integrated. Each form of learning can be said to comprise a set of learning strategies which are the procedures the children adopt in order to learn something specific. Furthermore, each form of learning describes the organisational forms constructed or established by children in order to learn. These informal forms of learning can be very effective.

When a number of children of varying ages are gathered together, the children's own organisational hierarchy functions as a *learning hierarchy* where the youngest children learn from the older ones or the inexperienced learn from the experienced. Children often organise themselves such that the oldest or most competent child sits at the computer. Behind him/her is to be found a row of the next in line in terms of age or competency, while the youngest or least competent children will be found in a row at the back.

The rows in the hierarchy are a manifestation of an order of precedence in which age, knowledge, and ability are the parameters according to which the children position themselves. This order of precedence is characterised by the fact that the highest levels of verbal participation are observed among the children standing closest to the computer, while verbal participation is virtually non-existent among those farthest away. For the children standing farthest from the computer, observation forms the basic strategy for learning. The children establish and attach themselves to these learning hierarchies which can be more or less casual in terms of organisation. They discover that it is a way of learning in which direct observation, mimicry, experimentation, demonstration, dialogue, and discussion all have a part to play.

Lave and Wenger (2001) employ the concept of legitimate peripheral participation, the process by which the individual is gradually trained within the community. This concept is related to the principle of apprenticeship, where learning takes place governed by a master's mode of organisation. In the children's *own modes of organisation,* there exist a number of similarities with legitimate peripheral participation, but there is a significant difference in that the mode of organisation is set within the children's own culture, and they can decide themselves whether or not they will participate. This is not the case with an apprenticeship mode of organisation as it is set within a workplace where training and the division of labour are organised and controlled by the master.

In their use of digital media, children also establish *learning networks* which they use to develop strategies for seeking out knowledge, for sharing their knowledge with others, and for constructing new knowledge. A network can be described as a system of connections between units. The children's networks should not be understood, however, as formally established networks like those often found within adult culture, which are formed in relation to a particular subject matter or some form of professional competence; instead they are loosely connected, informal networks. Norbert Elias' theory of figurations is relevant here, in that he sees people as connected via chains of units which he terms *interdependencies* (van Krigen 2002). The individual children or groups are understood as interdependent, that is to say mutually dependent on one another, comprising units within the network. Elias uses another concept to signify networks called *figurations,* which he understands to be relational structures between social actors oriented towards and dependent upon each other (ibid.). When Elias uses figurations as a counterpart to networks, figuration is understood as a relatively small system of connections built up around mutually dependent individuals and groups that share shifting, asymmetrical balances of power.

Among the various figurations or networks which children take part in or construct, some gain the status of learning networks in relation to digital media; indeed, this is a method of learning that has been made notable by the digital media. These learning networks are of both a physical and a virtual character.

There are two methods of learning in the network: children may pass knowledge on to one another via the network which then becomes a part of their learning processes, or learning may be achieved through collaborative processes of construction within the network. The exchange of ideas and transmission of knowledge occurs partly in the physical fellowship around the computer, and partly via e-mail and mobile phone, as well as in chatrooms and various online discussion forums.

When children use a computer, to play a game together for example, a *community of learning* is often formed around the computer; learning becomes a vital element of this community as it constitutes a *means* of enabling action within the game.

Etienne Wenger's concept of a *community of practice* is relevant here, as the children's learning communities are associated with a practice. Wenger's theory has been developed on the basis of the learning which occurs within the workplace; like workplace learning, children's learning communities are also a *means* of doing something, such as creating a product or a project. Attention is directed towards the context and the focus is on the fact that learning occurs within everyday practice. The community of practice is defined by Wenger and others as a group of individuals who share an undertaking, a penchant for a particular topic, or a set of problems, and who, through ongoing interaction, enhance their knowledge and expertise (Wenger, McDermott, & Snyder 2002).

If Wenger's theory is applied to children's learning communities, mutual engagement can be identified when the children draw upon, use, and are dependent upon each other's knowledge, e.g., when they need to learn how to use a new computer program or game. Within the community, the participants often also develop a shared repertoire in the form of certain actions, words, and forms of humour which become part of their communication. These communities can be either transitory or long-lasting. Learning is an integral element, with the learning processes primarily associated with joint performance, experimentation, comparison, dialogue, and discussion.

These informal forms of learning have proven effective ways to learn within, as well as outside of, school contexts where they have been applied (Sørensen & Audon 2004). It can therefore be fruitful to take them into consideration in the didactic design of serious games, whether in terms of the design of the games themselves or of the context for their usage.

6. PEDAGOGICAL APPROACHES

The concept of educational design also draws on various pedagogical approaches such as project pedagogy and Computer Supported Collaborative Learning (CSCL).

Within project pedagogy, there is particular focus on problem definition and solution, participation, and participant guidance as these aspects emphasise the learner's production and active participation. The concept of gaming in itself invites participation and participant guidance, which can be manifested in a wide variety of different ways. Many games are based around the construction of problems which the pupils are expected to solve. It is also possible to work with a design in which the pupils themselves construct problems for other pupils to solve.

CSCL is a research approach concerned with examining how the organisation of pupil collaboration can represent a fruitful path to learning. The concept *Thinking Together,* which has been developed within the computer-supported collaborative learning tradition, focuses on pupils' dialogue as an element of collaborative learning processes (Littleton et al. 2005). Neil Mercer and Rupert Wegrif (1999) address the relationship between learning and collaboration with a focus on dialogue; exploratory dialogue in particular is seen as essential for collaboration, and for the learning process and its outcomes. In exploratory dialogue, the pupils present hypotheses, challenge one another, and discuss, and the working process progresses on the basis of a joint acceptance of the proposals. In terms of the use of games within teaching and learning contexts, these theories are extremely relevant, especially for designing dialogues about subject-related content *during* the game and *after* the game: the teacher's discussion of subject-related content plays a vital role by encouraging the development of an explorative dialogue.

The part of the learning process which is set within the context, i.e. in connection with the game, is often invaluable for reflection, and thereby for the learning outcome. Kurt Squire's studies of Civilization III within an educational setting show that dynamic learning opportunities are created in connection with the game which engage the pupils and enrich classroom discourse by provoking discussion and requiring the pupils to reflect upon and develop their arguments (Squire 2004).

7. PLAY THEORY

Research in the field of developmental psychology has often regarded play as an instrument for child development and learning. However, there has been a break with this view as, within culturally-oriented, phenomeno-logical, and anthropological research, as well as in areas of recent psychological research, play is understood as a human mode of being with a meaning of its own (Sutton-Smith 1997). Johan Huizinga argues that there is a connection between play and culture. He considers play the origin of cultural development as culture is developed in and as play (Huizinga 1958). Furthermore, play is not only associated with children, but with humanity. *Homo Ludens: A Study of the Play-Element in Culture* is the title of the book in which he defines play as a voluntary act or activity which unfolds within certain predetermined spatial and temporal boundaries and which, as such, is a goal in itself. It is performed in accordance with binding rules and is accompanied by a sense of excitement and joy at the feeling of there being something other and more than "regular2 life (ibid.). Players play in order to enter the playing situation, which in itself constitutes the goal of the activity.

The concept of "play culture" has become central in Scandinavian child and youth research as a frame of understanding for the everyday lives of children and young people (Mouritzen 1996, Juncker 2006). Here, it is more a case of learning being understood as an instrument for the development of play competencies. This reversed means-end relationship has proven constructive for a theoretical understanding of learning processes in relation to computer games and digital media in general (Jessen 2001), primarily because it establishes an approach capable of examining these processes as goal-oriented learning.

Using this approach, a five-year project called *Children Growing up with Interactive Media –in a Future Perspective* examined children's everyday lives with digital media in order to identify what children attach particular importance to when participating in activities such as chat, computer games, website production, searching for information, etc. A near-field, theoretically-considered study was conducted of children in the home, in recreation centres, at schools, and at the library, focusing on children's relationships with one another and their use of artefacts, as well as the change processes which occur during their everyday lives. The results of this study indicate that children attach particular importance to (Sørensen 2002, Sørensen, Audon, & Levinsen 2010):

- Action – to do something oneself and take control
- Challenge – to be faced with problems, or outline them oneself, which need to be solved
- Reification – to create, produce, and experiment
- Sociality – to communicate and take part in communities
- Achievement – to receive recognition and respect
- Self-interpretation – to explore and experiment with one's identity, including gender
- Pleasure – to take part in situations providing sensory and bodily enjoyment

The play dimension forms part of the concept, as play is a pleasure-driven activity that can provide the impetus for participation in serious games. The set of terms outlined above expand upon what it is that children find pleasurable in their play activities and what would therefore seem to be productive if incorporated into the educational design of serious games.

8. COMPUTER GAME THEORY

Although computer games have been around for quite a while, they have only recently become the subject of a defined field of research. Computer games can be considered from various perspectives: as media, culture, narrative, or experience. Theoretically speaking, this necessitates an interdisciplinary approach, and this includes the consideration of learning games (Egenfeldt-Nielsen 2007). Games designed to be used in an educational setting belong to a genre which has emerged from entertainment-oriented computer games on the basis of the assumption, as previously mentioned, that such games contain an untapped potential which can be put to use in educational and learning contexts. As such, one key question is: what is this untapped potential? Several researchers have focused on this question. A recently conducted review on the learning outcomes of computer games within educational contexts during the period 1992-2007 concluded that computer games facilitate learning (ibid.). However, the related questions of who, what, why, and where are, according to the review, unclear (ibid.).

Paul Gee, who researches the learning potential of computer games, has assembled a list of characteristic features in the design of computer games which seem to be of particular interest from an educational design perspective. These features include:

- *Interactivity* – The interaction between player and interface and between the various participants is crucial. The more open the game is, the better the participant's opportunities for interpreting and producing and thereby gaining a feeling of ownership and control of the game.
- *Adaptation* – Some games provide the opportunity for learning in different ways that can be adapted to the various players' ways of learning.
- *Strong identity* – Identity is linked to a particular virtual character which can be more or less malleable to the fantasies, desires, and whims of the player. Identity is also closely linked to the functions, skills, and objectives to be enacted within the virtual world.
- *Well-ordered problems* – Problems in a good game are well-ordered in terms of the game's various levels such that the problems to be solved escalate from the simple to the more complex.
- *Frustrating in a good way* – Good games adjust the degree of difficulty and provide feedback so that players find the game challenging while receiving feedback on their progress.
- *Cycle of expertise* – Good games have an in-built system of repetition of learned practice and testing of competencies that equips the player for new challenges within the game.
- *Depth and fairness* – A game has depth when its elements appear straightforward and easy to learn while becoming increasingly complex as the player increases his/her level of understanding and ability. A game is fair when it is challenging, but put together in a way which makes success possible. (Gee 2007a).

According to Gee, these are among the fundamental characteristics in the design of many computer games which also seem crucial to effective learning (Gee 2007a).

9. COMMUNICATION AND MULTIMODALITY

When digital technology is coupled with game and play theory within an educational and learning perspective, the choice and combination of systems of expression, interactivity, and patterns of communication are key. As such, semiotic theory regarding communication and modality becomes relevant; this theory sees communication as a dynamic process situated within a socially and culturally constructed world (Kress 1993, Kress & van Leeuwen 2001).

The technological development has made multimodality topical. The term 'modality' stems from the Latin *modus*, meaning 'way'. Gunter Kress defines modality as "a culturally and socially fashioned resource for representation and communication" (Kress 2003, 45). The concept of multimodality can be defined as the creation of meaning by an utterance or text through a combination of different modalities (Løvland 2006, 26). In other words, it is the material forms, such as images (both living and static), sounds (music, speech, and noise), written texts, and graphic illustrations, which, along with their culturally and socially generated organisation, are central to the generation of meaning.

In schools, verbal language has traditionally played a dominant role. In recent years, the use of digital technology has changed this. Serious games make use of both individual forms of expression, or modalities, and the integration of several modalities. The modalities play a central role in the organisation of the subject-related content mediated by the game. From a design perspective, this requires a degree of insight into the unique characteristics of the various modalities. What is characteristic for images, words, and sounds? What are they particularly well-suited, and indeed unsuited, to communicating and mediating in a learning perspective? When images, words, and sounds are integrated, it results in new possibilities for communication and mediation. For example, it makes a difference whether a photo is used with or without a voiceover and whether an animation is used with or without music. The coupling of modalities provides different learning opportunities.

In the design processes, consideration must be given to whether each modality should remain separate or be combined with another form of expression, and if so, which one. When two forms of expression are combined, a new, integrated expression emerges which is something both different and more than the two individual modalities. For example, when an animation is set to music, the music governs perception of the animation. In the development of serious games, these combinations need to be tested from a learning perspective. Choices relating to the various modalities (colours, shapes, figures, typographies, sound effects, movements, etc.) are all communicative factors which supplement and influence the content being mediated (Thorlacius 2002).

10. CHILDREN AND CHILDREN POSITIONED AS PUPILS

When the learners are children, they are positioned within the school as pupils and, in terms of didactic category, are often considered on the basis of a developmental psychology approach. Developmental psychology has functioned as an important theoretical foundation for how teaching and learning processes are organised, and for how the category of pupil abilities has been viewed. The cognitive foundation of these theories with regard to learning is one way of perceiving and understanding children and young people.

When digital media gain a footing within schools, new anthropological, sociological, and cultural theories regarding children's usage of digital media become central. This is especially true of theories concerning children's games, play, and communication (Drotner 2001, Livingstone & Moria 2001, Jessen 2001, Sørensen, Jessen, & Olesen 2002, Stald 2009). These theories demonstrate that digital media have contributed to the creation of new conditions for children's everyday lives which influence the pupils' digital competencies and the expectations with which they are met at school.

To study children's cultures is to study a moving target (Livingstone & Bovill 1998). The target continuously shifts as media are subject to rapid technological change resulting in new usage patterns, as children constantly form new relations and activities. With digitalisation, the technology changes: new services and programs are developed, new multimodal forms emerge, media are used in new ways, and the social processes involved are altered within a global perspective. Children's usage of media does not take place as a series of isolated activities open to analysis only in terms of the relationship between child and medium. Children's media activities are both complex and integrated into their everyday lives. Ethnographically-inspired cultural theories focus on the creation of meaning based on the children and young people's own perspectives. Meaning-making is both an individual and a social process in which the individual child constantly negotiates and adjusts his or her understandings through interactions with other people and artefacts within various social and cultural spaces. From an educational design perspective relating to serious games developed for both formal and informal educational settings, it is vital to operate with the categories of both "pupils" and "children". In formal educational settings, children are positioned as pupils with a particular relationship to the teacher. The educational design for informal settings must meanwhile be crafted so as to allow children to play and work independently with the game.

11. TECHNOLOGY

The technology aspect is inevitably central to the educational design from the very beginning of the development process. Aside from the technological platform, which is also the basis for individual serious games, it also becomes important to consider the technologies that, from a pedagogical perspective, can be connected to the task when the game is used in a school context. For example, it may be appropriate for the pupils to work with e.g. blogs or other technologies in addition to the game, if this can support the learning process or provide improved learning results.

During the further development of new versions of a game, it is also essential to note possible technology innovations which may be inspirational. In the case of the development of the game Mingoville to Mingoville Virtual World, the inspiration came from social media, which interest many children. The characters from Mingoville School, where were created right at the beginning of the development of the game, were improved to become avatars that pupils could construct in collaboration with others through English communication. These activities were established and selected based on experiences with social media, combined with considerations about whether they would function as a way of teaching a foreign language.

12. THE ROLE OF THE TEACHER

It is clear from the findings of the *Serious Games on the Global Market Place* project that the role and positions of the teacher need to be incorporated into the game's didactic design to a greater degree than is the case at present. The game's educational design includes the learning objectives, the selection of subject-related content, planning, and the organisation of the arena for teaching and learning activities including pupil and teacher activities within the game itself. Until now, the designs of serious games have generally neglected the teacher in favour of pupil activities (See Hanghøj & Brund and Meyer & Sørensen in this book).

As such, there exists a challenge in designing serious games so as to be of interest not only to the pupils, but also to the teacher. In other words, the target audience for serious games intended for school settings is both pupils *and* teachers: games should be designed so that teachers see them as relevant to their teaching.

A number of studies have shown that teachers are frequently not actively engaged in teaching when games are used in lessons, as they often rely on the pupils' ability to manage by themselves based on the fact that pupils seem to be active and focused. At the same time, studies show that the teacher's role is imperative to the learning outcomes of the pupils, and that pupils are frequently critical of teachers' non-participation (Hanghøj & Brund 2010, Egenfeldt-Nielsen 2007, Sørensen & Audon 2004).

It is vital that serious games are not considered in isolation from other forms of teaching and learning practice, but rather as a supplement to and/ or integral part of this practice. Context and practice are key parameters for understanding the barriers and possibilities facing serious games. In addition, the role of the teacher is crucial to serious games as the teacher develops new educational functions and new positions in relation to the pupils.

When pupils use serious games, as well as other digital learning materials, the teacher frequently functions as "physically present, but professionally absent", which is to say that although the teacher is physically and socially present, he or she does not play an active, interventional role in the pupils' subject-related activities (Sørensen, Audon, & Levinsen 2010). As mentioned previously, the teacher often only becomes active when the game is over and the subject-related learning outcomes of the game are evaluated.

In a number of serious games, the consideration given to the teacher is limited to the inclusion of a set of teacher instructions, like those found in printed teaching materials. In Mingoville, there is a teacher figure or avatar integrated into the game; however this character cannot be controlled by the actual teacher present in the classroom. In Global Conflicts, there are no teacher avatars.

The teacher could be more actively incorporated into the educational design of games in a number of ways. Within the game itself, the teacher could feature as an avatar. For example, in Global Conflicts, the teacher could be included as an editor avatar that is in contact with the pupils' journalist avatars throughout the process. The teacher's role can be changed from peering over shoulders and functioning as assessor and summariser to playing an active part of the game with the design of an avatar to be played by the teacher.

This would allow the teacher to follow the pupils' learning processes in the game and, within the game's arena, to intervene with his or her subject-related knowledge and encourage pupils to think harder, when necessary, about what they are doing. The teacher would therefore be able to contribute to an on-going qualification of the pupils' learning processes.

The teacher could also be included by, for example, giving him or her certain special functions in relation to the game which are crucial for how the game plays out in the specific context. This might involve seeking out texts, images, or video clips related to the theme or semiotic domain involved, and matching the task to the specific age group and abilities of the class. As such, the teacher would be able to situate the game within the perspective and framework of their own teaching.

When serious games have been designed so as to provide teachers with clear possibilities for intervening in various ways with the learning processes of specific pupils and with the topic addressed by the game, it increases the likelihood of them finding games relevant to their lessons and allowing them to be actively, professionally present.

13. CONTEXT

Context is found in the model's outer layer. Aspects of context have been taken into consideration earlier in this article as they affect many of the model's other elements. Here, 'context' is understood as the learning environment which frames the game; the 'learning environment' is broadly defined as the physical surroundings in which learning takes place, which includes furniture, various other learning and everyday articles, and digital media, both software and hardware. The people involved, both pupils and teachers, and the ways in which they organise themselves as participants in teaching and learning processes are also key factors. A learning environment, as such, consists of a complex interplay between physical and technological settings, objects, participants, and activities. The context frames the way in which the game is used and has considerable significance for the game's learning potential (Squire 2004). This understanding of context obviously refers to a formal educational system, but a learning environment can also exist in the home where key figures, apart from the children, might be parents and siblings.

14. CONCLUSION

The educational design of serious games involves determining which elements can and should be included in the development of these games. The balance between the various elements is determined entirely by the game's subject-related content, the target group, and the formal and/or informal context for which the game is intended. The starting point has to be the subject-related content. Our examination of the global market demonstrates that, for a game to be incorporated within an educational context, the subject-related content needs to be clearly linked to the curriculum. In some cases, games are conceived on the basis of certain narrow traditions for teaching the subject at hand. Where such subject-specific traditions for teaching and learning exist, it is possible for serious games to offer new approaches; game and play-based approaches can present opportunities for breaking with traditions by introducing and working with subject-related content in new ways. The target group should be considered alongside the context: if the game has been developed for use entirely within a school context, its target group is comprised of teachers and pupils. As mentioned previously, it is crucial that such games be designed not only for pupils and groups of pupils, but also for teachers; the designer should consider teachers' varying backgrounds and abilities, their possibilities for acting within the game, and their interaction both within the game and in relation to the game. If the game has been developed for use within an informal context, the user group is frequently limited to children and young people. In certain instances, parents may take part and assume a sort of teacher role, particularly in the case of younger children. In this situation, it may be appropriate to compose some form of paratext (Genette 1987), for example a parental guide concerning the game's possible applications.

REFERENCES

Bolter, J. D. 1999. "Remediation and the Desire and Immediacy." Paper presented at the conference on Creativity & Comsumption, University of Luton, March 29-31.

Chen, C. & A. McFarlane. 2007. "Gaming Culture and digital Literacy: Inspiration and Audience." In *Digital kompetense. Nordic Journal of Digital Literacy*. Oslo: Oslo University Press.

Dale, E. L. 1989. *Pedagogisk Profesjonalitet*. Oslo: Gyldendal.

Dale, E. L. 2000. "Professionalisering og læring i organisasioner." In *Innovation, kompetence, læring*, edited by P. Andersen and P. Frederiksen. Frederiksberg: Dafolo.

Danbolt, G. & Å Enerstvedt. 1995. Når voksenkultur og barns kultur møtes. Evalueringsrapport. Oslo.

Drotner, K. 2001. *Medier for fremtiden: børn, unge og det nye medielandskab*. Copenhagen: Høst.

Egenfeldt-Nielsen, S. 2005. "Can Education and Psychology Join Forces. The Clash of Benign and Malign Learning from Computer Games." *Nordicom Review* 2.

Egenfeldt-Nielsen, S. 2007. "Overview of research on the educational use of video games." In *Digital kompetense. Nordic Journal of Digital Literacy*. Oslo: Oslo University Press.

Gee, J. P. 2007a. *What Video Games Have to Teach Us about Learning and Literacy*, rev. ed. New York: Palgrave Macmillan.

Gee, J. P. 2007b. "Are Video Games Good for Learning?" In *Digital kompetense. Nordic Journal of Digital Literacy*. Oslo: Oslo University Press.

Hanghøj, T. & E. B. Christian. 2010. "Teacher Roles and Positionings in Relation to Educational Games" Paper presented at the 4th European Conference on Game-Based Learning, Danmarks Pædagogiske Universitetsskole, October 21-22.

Hermansen, M. 2001. *Læringens univers*, 4th ed. Aarhus: Forlaget Klim.

Hiim, H. & E. Hippe. 2000 (Norwegian edition 1993). *Læring gennem oplevelse, forståelse og handling. En studiebog i didaktik*. Copenhagen: Gyldendal.

Hopman, S. & K. Riguarts, eds. 1995. *Didaktik and/or Curriculum*. Kiel: IPN.

Huizinga, J. 1958. *Homo Ludens. Om kulturens oprindelse i leg*. Copenhagen: Gyldendal.

Illeris, K. 1999. *Læring – aktuel læringsteori i spændingsfeltet mellem Piaget, Freud og Marx*. Frederiksberg: Roskilde University Press.

Illeris, K. 2006. *Læring*. Roskilde: Roskilde University Press.

Jessen, C. 2001. *Børn, leg og computerspil*. Odense: Odense University Press.

Juncker, B. 2006. *Om processen – Det æstetiskes betydning i børns kultur*. Tiderne Skifter.

Kress, G. 1993. Communication and Culture. Australia: New South Wales University Press.

Kress, G. & T. van Leeuwen. 2001. *Multimodal Discourse. The Modes and Media of Contemporary Communication*. London: Cappelen.

Kress, G. 2003. *Literacy in the New Media Age*. London: Routledge.

Lave, J. & E. Wenger. 1991. *Situated Learning: Legitimate Peripheral Participation*. New York: Cambridge University Press.

Livingstone, S. & B. Moria, eds. 2001. *Children and their Changing Media Environment: A European Comparative Study*. New York: Erlbaum.

Mercer, N. & R. Wegrif. 1999. "Is 'exploratory talk' productive talk". In *Learning with computers. Analysing productive interaction*, edited by K. Littleton & P. Light. London; New York: Routledge.

Mouritsen, F. 1996. *Legekultur. Essays om børnekultur, leg og fortælling*. Odense.

Schnack, K. 2000. *Er didaktik og curriculum det samme?* Copenhagen: Danmarks Pædagogiske Universitet.

Selfton-Green, J. 2006. *Literature review in informal learning with technology outside school: A report for nesta futurelab*. Bristol: NESTA Futurelab.

Shaffer, K.D. 2006. *How Computer Games Help Children Learn*. Palgrave Macmillan.

Squire, K. 2002. *Rethinking the role of games in education*. Game Studies 2(1).

Squire, K. 2004. "Replaying history." PhD Diss., Indiana University.

Sutton-Smith, B. 1997. *The Ambiguity of Play*. Cambridge, Mass.: Harvard University Press.

Sørensen, B. H. 2009a. "Didaktisk design för 'seriösa spel.'" In *Didaktisk design i digital miljö: nye möjligheter för lärande*, edited by S. Selander & E. Svärdemo-Åberg, 172-185. Stockholm: Liber.

Sørensen, B. H. 2009b. "Concepts of Educational Design for Serious Games." In *Research, Reflections and Innovations in Integrating ICT in Education*, 278-282. Lissabon: FORMATEX.

Sørensen, B. H. 2002. "Børns nye læringsforudsætninger – didaktiske perspektiver." In *Børn på nettet*, edited by B. H. Sørensen, C. Jessen, & B. R. Olesen. Kommunikation og læring. Copenhagen: Gads Forlag.

Sørensen, B. H., C. Jessen, & B. R. Olesen. 2002. *Børn på nettet*. Kommunikation og læring. Copenhagen: Gads Forlag.

Sørensen, B. H. & L. Audon. 2004. "Nye Læringsformer og rum – digitale medier i vidensamfundets skole. Forskningsrapport." Copenhagen: Danmarks Pædagogiske Universitet.

Sørensen, B. H. & B. Meyer. 2010. "Design for game based learning platforms: in a global perspective." In *Proceedings of Society for Information Technology & Teacher Education International Conference 2010*, edited by D. Gibson & B. Dodge, 2071-2078. Chesapeake, VA: AACE.

van Krieken, R. 2002. *Norbert Elias*. Copenhagen: Hans Reitzels Forlag.

Wenger, E. 1998. *Communities of Practice. Learning, Meaning, and Identity*. Cambridge: Cambridge University Press.

Wenger, E., R. McDermott, & W. M. Snyder. 2002. *Cultivating Communities of Practice: A guide to Managing Knowledge*. Boston: Harvard Business School Publishing.

4. TEACHERS AND SERIOUS GAMES

4 A. TEACHER ROLES AND POSITIONINGS IN RELATION TO EDUCATIONAL GAMES

Thorkild Hanghøj & Christian Engel Brund

1. INTRODUCTION

Despite the fact that research on educational games has been conducted for more than forty years, the actual practices of *teaching* with games is still largely overlooked. Instead, the research on educational games has mostly been driven by *determinist* and *essentialist* approaches that aim either to measure the learning outcomes of different forms of game-based learning or to identify the inherent learning potential of particular game designs (Hanghøj 2008). As a consequence, the actual practices and processes of teaching with games have only received limited attention from researchers (e.g. Dorn 1989, Squire 2004, Egenfeldt-Nielsen 2005, Sandford et al. 2006, Hanghøj 2008, Magnussen 2008, Simpson & Stansberry 2008, Williamson 2009, Van Eck 2009). However, many of these attempts only provide limited descriptions of the pedagogical choices and considerations that teachers make when they teach with games. This lack of empirical knowledge about how and why teachers use games is quite striking, given the fact that teachers are crucial gatekeepers when it comes to actually selecting, enacting, and evaluating educational games as a part of their teaching. This paper consequently attempts to describe how and for what reasons teachers bring games into classrooms, and how this creates problems and opportunities in relation to existing teaching practices. More specifically, we seek to explore three interrelated research questions. First of all, what roles do teachers assume when they facilitate educational games? Secondly, how do teachers position themselves in relation to educational games? And thirdly, how can we understand the relationship between game-based teaching practices and particular game designs?

2. TEACHER ROLES

In order to answer these questions, we will first present the findings from a research project on an ICT-supported debate game, which indicate that game-based teaching involves a shift between different "teacher roles" (Hanghøj 2008). Next, we will analyse whether this description of roles can be useful for understanding game-based teaching with a series of educational computer games entitled Global Conflicts (GC), which represents a rather different game format with different "modalities" – i.e. modes of communication (Kress 2010). Our analysis suggests that it is difficult to understand why and how the teachers used the computer games with only an analysis of the teachers' interactional roles. Instead, we try to account for the ways in which teachers "positioned" themselves in relation to the GC games (Herrlitz, Ongstad, & van de Ven 2007). Combining these perspectives, game-based teaching can be understood as a complex series of pedagogical choices, practices, and meaning-making processes, which can be analysed through the complimentary notions of teacher roles, game modalities, and positionings.

From our perspective, game-based teaching should not be understood as a "fixed" practice as it involves a repertoire of shifting teacher roles. The term "teacher role" is commonly used among educational researchers and practitioners to describe how teachers respond to various demands and situations. Inspired by the work of Mead and Goffman, we will conceptualise teacher roles from an *interactionist* perspective (Atkinson & Housley 2003). A role can be defined as: "the normative expectation of situationally specific meaningful behaviour" (Joas 1993, 226). Following this definition, teacher roles are continually configured and re-configured in relation to the situated enactment of mutual norms and expectations. Thus, we conceive of teacher roles as a relational property of social interaction within a classroom context. This means that teacher roles should not be seen as fixed "scripts" or functions, but rather as more or less stable patterns of interaction and expectations that are based upon *processes of continual negotiation* – i.e. between a teacher, a game scenario, and his or her students.

So far, there have been few empirical studies of how educational gaming requires different or changed teacher roles. One exception is Hanghøj's study of how a group of Danish social studies teachers enacted The Power Game, which is an ICT-supported debate game on parliamentary election designed for social studies education in Danish upper secondary schools (Hanghøj 2008). In the study, Hanghøj identified three different pedagogical approaches to the same game scenario. One teacher mainly viewed the game scenario as a "script" to be followed, and described her own role as a "puppet" and had difficulties "seeing herself" in the game. Two teachers followed a "performative" approach by emphasising the "entertainment value" of the students' role-playing abilities. Finally, two other teachers were mainly "explorative" in their approach and focused on the students' ability to "build hypotheses" in relation to the election scenario – i.e. why did the students favour certain key political issues instead of others? All the teachers also changed approaches, which implies that game-based teaching requires teachers to master a repertoire of different roles.

Based upon Hanghøj's findings, it can be argued that teachers change back and forth between four different roles when they facilitate games for educational purposes, namely by performing as *instructor, playmaker, guide*, and *evaluator*. The role of "instructor" concerns teachers' attempts to plan and communicate the overall goals of a game scenario in relation to particular learning objectives. This role is also an integrated part of most teachers' everyday practices – i.e. when giving overt instruction in relation to a particular school subject (cf. Alexander 2008). The "playmaker" role refers to teachers' ability to communicate the tasks, roles, goals, and dynamics of a particular game scenario as seen from a player perspective (cf. Hanghøj 2008). The role of the "guide" encapsulates how teachers support or "scaffold" students in their attempts to meet particular learning objectives when they play a game (cf. Wood et al. 1976). Games also require teachers to perform as "evaluators" in order to understand, explore, and provide dialogical response to the students' experiences of playing a game – as seen from an outsider's perspective (cf. Wegerif 2007). These four teacher roles should not be understood as "ideal types" or as normative goals for teaching with games. Rather, they can be seen as pragmatic categories based upon empirical analysis of teachers' game-based practices. Because of this, the roles and their relationship are open to discussion and further analysis.

3. CASE: THE GLOBAL CONFLICTS SERIES

Inspired by the four game-based teacher roles described above, we have tried to explore whether they can be used to understand game-based teaching in relation to game formats other than ICT-supported debate games. More specifically, we both took part in a research project on the use of educational computer games, in which we studied how teachers use different games in the Global Conflicts (GC) series. The GC games, which currently include 12 different missions, have been designed to be used both in secondary and upper secondary schools (age group 13-17). Each of the missions are set in a 3D environment, where the student plays a character (i.e. a freelance journalist or a UN representative), who has to explore particular issues and conflicts in different regions of the world – i.e. illegal immigration across the US-Mexican border or the use of child soldiers in Uganda. This is done by "interviewing" different characters within a given a timeframe and collecting "counter-arguments", which must be used in a confrontational interview with responsible authorities such as a factory owner or a mayor waiting at the end of a mission. The game scenario then concludes with an evaluation of the student's ability to find and use arguments properly.

Using several cycles of research, we have generated comprehensive data that documents how different versions of the GC games have been adopted by 19 teachers distributed across ten different secondary schools located in three different countries (Denmark, Norway, and England). In some cases, the teachers were asked to teach with a game in relation to a specific purpose as part of a design intervention – i.e. to explore how the students' game experiences could be transformed into journalistic articles (Hanghøj 2010). In other cases, the teachers were explicitly asked to select and teach with the GC games in relation to their own purposes with only a minimum of interference from the researchers during the preparation phase. On average, each game session lasted approximately 90 minutes and was integrated with other relevant activities such as reading relevant background material prior to the game, classroom discussion of the themes explored in a particular mission, and/or written assignments. Only a few of the teachers were experienced gamers and none of them had previous experience with teaching the GC games. Most of the game sessions were documented through video observations and field notes. Moreover, each game session was followed by post-game interviews with the participating teachers, which mainly focused on the teachers' experience of teaching with the game and how this experience could be related to their everyday teaching practices.

4. GAME MODALITIES AND TEACHER ROLES

Taken at a general level, the game sessions with the GC games roughly followed a similar pattern. All the teachers had prepared themselves for the game sessions, they all introduced the game scenarios, and they all rounded the game sessions off with some form of classroom discussion. At the same time, there were striking differences between the communicative patterns in the debate game sessions previously mentioned and the GC sessions. First of all, having completed the initial teacher introductions and the log-in procedures to the game, which were often accompanied by technical barriers, there was a remarkably low level of audible sound in all the GC game sessions. Even though many teachers divided the students into pairs to promote discussion, there was quite limited dialogue between the students, who sat facing the screen and focused their attention on reading and exploring different forms of game information. Consequently, most of the dialogue consisted of relatively closed questions that related to the way the students "interviewed" the game characters – i.e. "should I click on this or that question?" The most frequent sounds audible during the game sessions were the in-game sounds, humming computers, and mouse clicking.

Secondly, there was also quite limited communication between students and teachers, who spent most of the game time simply observing how the students played the game. Some students would ask the teachers to help them in order to proceed in the game, especially students who experienced difficulties with reading the relatively large amount of text in the game. In the post-game interviews, several teachers described how they had assumed the role of somebody who "looked over the shoulders" of the students. To some teachers, this was clearly seen as a drawback of the game. As an example, one teacher felt that it was quite "boring" to teach with the game and contrasted the GC game with the ICT-supported educational role-playing game *Homicide*, for which the teacher role was much more demanding but also more rewarding (cf. Magnussen 2008). At the same time, she also described how the reduced role of the teacher could be seen as a "strength" of the game design since the game could easily be played by a "substitute teacher" with "very little preparation". Another teacher described a similar ambivalence when guiding the students. For him, it was a positive value that the students' self-directed game activities challenged teachers' natural tendencies to be "control freaks". On the other hand, he also found it quite difficult "to get an overview" of the students' actual game decisions, which made it hard to scaffold them as they progressed through different trajectories within game scenario. Overall, many of the teachers felt that the game design made them assume relatively passive roles with limited overview and limited possibilities for interacting or guiding the students. Similarly, when the teachers conducted the end-of-game discussions, they made very few references to actual game events.

However, there was at least one exception to this overall description of the teachers' facilitation of the GC games. More specifically, Mark, an ICT teacher who played computer games on a regular basis and taught game design both at secondary and upper secondary levels, chose a rather different approach when teaching with the game. After he had introduced the game and the students had started playing, Mark observed that some students made very slow progress. As a result, he interrupted the game activities and emphasised the limited in-game time as an important aspect of the game dynamics. In Mark's words, the students should not spend all their time on asking questions in the beginning of the game, but carefully consider when and whom to ask the right questions. In several other game sessions, the teachers did not explain this time aspect of the game to the students, which meant that many of them had no clear idea of the strategic aspects involved and ended up using all their time working through the beginning of the game. In addition to this, Mark also reacted promptly when he observed how a group of students, which he later termed "lower ability boys", refrained from reading the text in the game and simply clicked randomly on the dialogue boxes in order to complete the game as fast as possible. This pattern of behaviour was quite common in almost all the game sessions and was also commented upon by several teachers in the post-game interviews. However, when Mark observed this pattern spread among some of the boys, he promptly interrupted the game and asked the boys to stop "turning the game into a click-a-thon". Later on, when one of the boys continued the "click-a-thon", he was expelled from the class for playing the game in an inappropriate way. As these examples suggest, Mark assumed the role of an active playmaker by trying to make the goals and rules of the game scenario visible to the students.

The point here is not whether Mark facilitated the game in a "correct" or "incorrect" way. Our point is simply that Mark was the only teacher who actively intervened with phenomena he observed during the students' actual game play. One obvious explanation for Mark's interference with the game activities could be that he was quite a "game competent" teacher, who had a lot of experience with playing, designing, and teaching computer games. Thus, Mark was less fascinated or intimidated by the GC games as an unfamiliar technology. As mentioned above, many other teachers were unable or unwilling to engage with the students' game activities. It may be argued that the GC games represented a multimodal form of inquiry, which only marginally afforded teachers opportunities for assuming active roles during the actual game activities (Kress 2010). The communicative modes of the GC games (3D visual representations, texts in dialogue boxes, game sound) are screen-based and primarily intended for single-player interaction. Moreover, there are no explicit references to teacher-driven activities within the game, which means that there are few incentives for teachers to be involved in the game activities or in the game evaluation of the students. Consequently, the affordances – or what might be termed the *pedagogical model* – of the GC games largely rendered the teachers superfluous during the game activities, unless they actively interrupted the students' experience of playing the game.

As the examples above suggest, the four game-based teacher roles mentioned earlier are only partially able to describe how the teachers in this study facilitated the *GC* games. Thus, even though all the teachers assumed the role of an instructor, the remaining three roles of guide, playmaker, and evaluator were much more weakly defined than in our earlier study of teachers' approaches to debate games (Hanghøj 2008). Mark"s approach to the GC games indicates that it was not impossible for teachers to assume more active roles during the game activities. However, for most of the teachers in this study, such practices were not employed as the design of the 5 GC games did not encourage an active teacher role. At the same time, many of the participating teachers had put a lot of effort into preparing how they intended to teach with the GC games, and they were all quite active at the beginning and the end of the game sessions.

5. TEACHER POSITIONINGS

In order to provide a more contextualised account of the teachers' experiences of teaching with the GC games, we will now describe how the teachers positioned themselves in relation to the game sessions. This part of the analysis focuses on a sub-set of our empirical data in which eight Danish teachers had been asked to teach with the GC games without interference from the researchers in the preparation phase. In analysing the eight pre-game teacher interviews, we have identified two analytical themes which we wish to discuss here. The first theme concerns the teachers' general motives for teaching with games. That is, the ways in which they positioned their teaching with games in relation to their everyday or general pedagogical approaches. The second theme concerns how the teachers positioned themselves in relation to the GC games and describes more specific pedagogical assumptions about how to make the game relevant or "visible" in relation to curricular knowledge aspects. These two analytical themes also represent a distinction between the teachers' *general* pedagogical approaches to teaching with games and more *specific* pedagogical approaches to teaching with the GC games.

5.1. WHY TEACH WITH GAMES?

In the interviews, all eight teachers mentioned that student motivation is one of their main reasons for teaching with games. Moreover, they also viewed games as a good way of providing variation from everyday forms of teaching, especially as an alternative to standard textbooks and more traditional forms of teaching. The teachers assumed that games were valuable methods for teaching as they might appeal to students other than those who would normally be interested in school activities. In addition to this, the teachers had different experiences with different types of games. Several teachers had used a lot of role-playing games and emphasised how these games were able to support more embodied forms of learning as well as provide new perspectives on a given topic. However, the teachers clearly differed in their experience with computer games and ICTs, which many of them bundled together in the same category. Moreover, the teachers' familiarity with ICTs and computer games turned out to be quite significant in relation to how they enacted (or failed to enact) the GC games and how they subsequently evaluated and reflected upon the game sessions. The teachers can be grouped into three categories that reflect how they positioned themselves in relation to teaching with computer games.

To four of the teachers, computer games represented a relatively unfamiliar but interesting form of teaching and learning, which they were curious to learn more about. These teachers viewed teaching with computer games as a way of fulfilling a larger demand of being able to teach with various forms of ICTs. Thus, Karin described how she "needed to be pushed" in relation to using ICTs. Similarly, Jens Christian mentioned ICTs as a barrier, which "needed to be overcome". As mentioned previously, the technical aspects became quite important for these four teachers when facilitating the GC games. Both Jens Christian and Kenneth experienced problems making the game run on the computers at their different schools. Similarly, both Karin and Kira mentioned that they depended entirely on technical help from their colleague Louis in order to run the game. It could be said that these four teachers positioned themselves as *interested, but insecure* about how to teach with computer games.

Two other teachers, Andreas and Kim, had a far more specific interest in teaching with computer games as they had experienced how this form of learning resonated with the students" own interests in playing games outside of school. As Andreas put it, "it is a bit worrying that there is not more focus on working with games, I mean, considering that so many [students] play in their leisure time". Both teachers had experience with various ways of teaching with COTS games in different school subjects such as Danish, English, and media – i.e. by letting students perform textual analysis of free online games, writing walk-throughs for games, or recording films of how they interacted within the gameworld of *World of WarCraft*. Moreover, these two teachers, who were responsible for introducing ICT and media at their school, were generally interested in helping their colleagues to overcome their "fear" of new technologies. We could say that they positioned themselves as having an *experimental* approach to game-based learning at many different levels –in relation to different types of COTS computer games, different curricular aims, and as a means for promoting collaboration with colleagues regarding media and ICTs.

The remaining two teachers, Dan and Louis, also had considerable ICT experience, but only had limited experience of teaching with computer games. In contrast to Andreas and Kim, they were not particularly interested in teaching with COTS computer games because these games were not designed for educational purposes. Instead, they were more interested in how educational computer games could be used for teaching about particular curricular concepts such as globalisation or the African continent. As such, these two teachers positioned themselves as adopting a more *pragmatic approach* to educational gaming, which weighed the pros and cons of how different educational games could be used to fulfil particular goals. As Louis put it: "There are some things which games can't do… you need to be careful not to turn the technology into something which takes over everything. There are some things which it makes more sense to do nice and quietly with a pen and paper".

5.2. MAKING THE GC GAMES VISIBLE

The teachers also positioned themselves in relation to more specific pedagogical approaches for teaching with the GC games. In other words, all the teachers explored ways of making the GC game scenarios "visible" in relation to particular curricular aims. In this respect, the teachers shared a number of assumptions. First of all, there was the assumption that the GC games should not stand alone, but should be integrated with other learning resources (i.e. film clips, texts on the internet, student assignments, etc.) and other teaching methods such as direct instruction or classroom discussions. Several teachers mentioned that the GC games could work as an introduction to a particular theme – i.e. when planning a theme week about the African continent. Moreover, all the teachers considered how the students should be organised when playing the game – i.e. whether they should play single-handedly or work in pairs. All the teachers also commented on the relatively large amount of text to be read within the game, which many of them expected to put off some of their students.

However, the eight teachers clearly differed when they described how they planned to teach with the GC games. It was quite clear that the four teachers who only had limited experience with computer games also had relatively vague or abstract ideas on how to make the GC games relevant in relation to particular aims. Thus, none of these teachers offered a detailed plan for relating the game scenario to particular curricular aims. Conversely, the two teachers who were interested in promoting game-based learning through COTS games were quite critical of the game design, as they expected that many of their students would "quickly see through the game" and its educational motives. Finally, Dan and Louis, who took a more pragmatic approach, provided relatively detailed descriptions of how the game scenario could fulfil curricular aims by integrating the game session with other teaching activities. To quote Louis, it was important that "the students' knowledge does not get stuck within the game".

6. CONCLUSION

The aim of this chapter has been to argue that game-based teaching is a complex phenomenon that must be understood in relation to social interaction (teacher roles), game design (modalities), and pedagogical approaches (positionings). Our analysis suggests that game-based teaching can be understood as a dynamic interplay between different teacher roles. However, depending on the modalities of a given game design, teachers may easily be rendered superfluous or forced to assume relatively passive roles. Moreover, our analysis indicates that teachers' familiarity with particular game formats and ICTs influences their abilities to plan and to make a game scenario become visible in relation to curricular as well as pedagogical aims. Given the crucial significance of the teacher as a professional practitioner in choosing, facilitating, and legitimising educational games, it is dangerously misleading to over-emphasise the importance of game design as an isolated aspect of educational gaming. Instead, we need much more contextualised research on how the pedagogical models of educational game scenarios are able – or unable – to be "translated" in relation to new and existing pedagogies.

REFERENCES

Alexander, R. 2008. *Essays on Pedagogy*. London: Routledge.

Atkinson, P. & W. Housley. 2003. *Interactionism. An Essay in Sociological Amnesia*. London: Sage.

Becker, K. 2008. "Video Game Pedagogy: Good Games = Good Pedagogy." In *Games: Purpose and Potential in Education*, edited by C. T. Miller. New York: Springer.

Dorn, J. 1989. "Simulation Games: One More Tool On the Pedagogical Shelf." *Teaching Sociology* 17(1): 1-18.

Egenfeldt-Nielsen, S. 2005. "Beyond Edutainment: The Educational Potential of Computer Games." PhD Diss., IT University of Copenhagen.

Gee, J. P. & J. L. Green. 1998. "Discourse Analysis, Learning, and Social Practice: A Methodological Study." *Review of Research in Education* 23: 119-169.

Hanghøj, T. 2008. "Playful Knowledge. An Explorative Study of Educational Gaming." PhD Diss., University of Southern Denmark.

Hanghøj, T. 2010. "Clashing and Emerging Genres: Teaching and playing educational computer games." Paper presented at the Designs for Learning conference, Stockholm, March 17-19.

Herrlitz, P., S. Ongstad, & P. van de Ven, eds. 2007. *Research on mother tongue education in a comprative international perspective*. Amsterdam: Rodopi.

Joas, H. 1993. *Pragmatism and Social Theory*. Chicago: University of Chicago Press.

Kress, G. 2010. *Multimodality: A social semiotic approach to contemporary communication*. London: Routledge.

Magnussen, R. 2008. "Representational Inquiry in Science Learning Games." PhD Diss., University of Aarhus.

Sandford, R., M. Ulicsak, K. Facer, & T. Rud. 2006. *Teaching with Games. Using commercial off-the-shelf computer games in formal education*. Research Report. Bristol: NESTA FutureLab.

Simpson, E. & S. Stansberry. 2008. "Video Games and Teacher Development: Bridging the Gap in the Classroom." In *Games: Purpose and Potential in Education*, edited by C. T. Miller. New York: Springer.

Smidt, J. 2002. "Double Histories in Multivocal Classrooms: Notes Toward an Ecological Account of Writing." *Written Communication* 19(3): 414-443.

Squire, K. 2004. "Replaying History. Learning World History through playing Civilization III." PhD Diss., Indiana University.

Van Eck, R. 2009. "A Guide to Integrating COTS Games into Your Classroom." In *Handbook of Research on Effective Electronic Gaming in Education*, Vol. 1, edited by R. Ferdig. New York: Information Science Reference.

Williamson, B. 2009. *Computer games, schools, and young people. A report for educators on using games for learning.* Bristol: NESTA FutureLab.

Wood, D., J. Bruner, & G. Ross. 1976. "The role of tutoring in problem solving." *Journal of child psychology and psychiatry* 17: 89-100.

4 B. EDUCATIONAL DESIGN FOR LEARNING GAMES WITH A FOCUS ON THE TEACHER'S ROLES

Birgitte Holm Sørensen & Bente Meyer

1. INTRODUCTION

In recent years, learning games have been the subject of growing attention. Learning games are generally designed in such a way that students are the only players; teacher involvement is usually limited to the paratexts, i.e. the guides and instructions, which accompany the games. In the project *Serious Games on the Global Market Place*, we investigate how two learning games, Mingoville and Global Conflicts, are used. Mingoville is an internet-based virtual universe that was originally developed for teaching English as a foreign language to beginners; in Denmark it is used in grades 3 and 4 (www.mingoville.com). Global Conflicts is an online 3D learning game which has been developed for cross-disciplinary courses of study for grades 8-12 (http://www.globalconflicts.eu/). Both these learning tools receive ongoing online development and are designed for a global market. As such, they join the growing array of digital learning tools, including learning games, which are marketed and used globally.

In the following, we will introduce Genette's concept of paratexts and its relevance and potential within an analysis and design perspective. Next, we will analyse the paratexts attached to Mingoville and Global Conflicts. Experiences regarding the role and positions of the teacher in relation to the usage of these two games will then be considered, incorporating experiences from the results of our research. These experiences indicate a demand for teachers to be assigned a more active role in the educational design of games. This point is discussed and a number of suggestions are put forward as to how teachers' roles and positions can be better incorporated within the educational design of games.

2. PARATEXTUAL ELEMENTS ACCORDING TO GENETTE

Paratext is the name given by the French structuralist Gerard Genette to phenomena and discourses that are liminal to texts of a certain status (i.e. works) but which serve to define them, explain them, or name them (Genette 1987). Paratexts are thus the titles, names, and pseudonyms, cover notes, blurbs, dedications, notes, prefaces, and postfaces that mediate the text 'itself' or constitute it within the world of texts. Genette states that paratexts in fact enable the text to become a book or work that can be offered to readers and the general public. Paratexts, though peripheral to the text itself, are therefore central to the life, reception, and contextualisation of the text (ibid.).

Genette offers several detailed descriptions of the role of paratexts, which are understood as situated in zones of transition and transaction between text and off-text. Thus, the paratext has spatial, temporal, substantial, pragmatic, and functional characteristics, which correspond to its position (*where?*), its date of appearance (*when?*), its (verbal) mode of existence (*how?*), its addressee (*to whom?*), and its message (*what is it good for?*). In relation to this paper all of these may be relevant; however, the position, addressee, and message will be most significant, as here the paratext is studied in the context of teacher roles in game-based learning. A central aspect of the pragmatic function of the paratext in relation to the teaching and learning perspectives of games is the idea, suggested by Genette, that paratexts have an illocutionary force, i.e. that they are performative in the sense that they inform, interpret, give advice about, or define the main text. The significance of informing teachers, giving them advice, and guiding them in connection with game-based learning, which often focuses primarily on the role of the learner, will be developed below.

3. PARATEXTUAL ASPECTS OF DIGITAL GAMES

In terms of the study of digital games and media, the use of Genette's concept of paratexts may be critiqued in the sense that Genette bases his theory on the idea of a main text and auxiliary paratexts, i.e. a holistic textual ideal; he is mostly concerned with verbal textual phenomena, and not for instance with visual media or technology, though he does mention that paratexts can be illustrations and that technical evolution will change the role of the paratext. As a consequence of these (historical) limitations of Genette's text, the idea and the role of the paratext has been reconceptualised in media studies by, among others, Lunenfeld (1999) and Consalvo (2007).

As suggested by Lunenfeld (1999), the aesthetic of digital media has an unfinished character, and the boundaries between text and context have therefore begun to dissolve as texts have, for instance, become hypertexted. Genette's theory of the paratext can in this context be understood as being very much limited to the terms of the publishing verbal textual industry, where the idea of the bounded work still prevails. What characterises digital media, in comparison (and in contrast to Genette's approach), is that digital forms are composed of the same streams of data, regardless of whether the information is textual, visual, or aural, etc. This means that in the age of digital media paratexts are no more easily distinguishable from the texts themselves, as the rigid demarcations between formerly discrete texts become fluid liminal zones. A similar critique or re-conceptualisation of Genette's concept is found in Consalvo (2007), which traces how, in a digital age in which gaming has gained increasing significance on the market, paratexts have become paratextual industries that surround and are integrated into gaming as a global culture. For Consalvo, paratexts are not peripheral to gaming itself, but are becoming still more integral to the gaming industry every year, for instance in the form of hints and cheats, and of various texts of advice, information, and instructions in connection with the social performance of game play, such as how to play a game properly or improperly. In this sense the text and the paratext have collapsed into a variety of social and commercial approaches to the gaming experience – that is, knowledge, for example of how to cheat or how not to cheat, is embedded into the actual activity of game play itself as a social and cultural phenomenon. As Consalvo argues, gaming capital is inherently paratextual, and is becoming indistinguishable from actual game-playing activity.

4. READING THE PARATEXTS OF MINGOVILLE

Paratextual elements serve the purpose, as stated by Genette, of introducing or presenting the text to the reader and to the public. As such, paratexts are generally auxiliary, subordinate to the text itself, which serves as their *raison d'être*. However, looking at game-based material that is published and accessed online, the role, and indeed the peripheral nature of the paratext is challenged and transformed, as argued above. This applies to game-based learning platforms for which paratextual elements serve both as external references or guidance to the proper or possible uses of the material, and exist as integrated elements in the platform. In the following we shall account for the paratextual elements of the game-based platforms www.mingoville. com and http://www.globalconflicts.eu/, both of which were studied in the Serious Games on a Global Market Place project. The purpose of pointing to the paratextual elements of this platform is, as mentioned above, to discuss how and why game-based learning material employs paratextuality to support and develop teacher roles in educational games.

Mingoville is a game-based learning platform in which children meet the Pinkeltons, who are citizens of the simulated world Mingoville – a city inhabited by flamingos. The main part of the platform (the Mingoville School) contains 10 Missions that take the learners through a variety of themes such as The Family, Colours and Clothes, Numbers, and Letters. These are basic areas for vocabulary acquisition defined in the national (Danish) curriculum for English and are conceptualised as central to primary education in English worldwide.

The platform has been in development since 2009 and now includes a Mingoville Virtual World, in which children can chat and play games online while using the vocabulary introduced in the Mingoville School zone. The Mingoville School and Mingoville Virtual World are different activity zones; users must choose to enter one or the other once they are logged onto the platform. Before logging on to the platform users are presented with the Mingoville concept and its educational principles on the Mingoville home page, where menus, testimonials, introductory texts, and videos point to the different functions and learning potentials of the platform. As a first encounter with Mingoville this 'main web page' has the role of a paratextual interface that introduces the main 'text' of Mingoville (i.e. the learning activities) to the 'reader' and the public. It is both this initial Mingoville interface and aspects of the activities in the Mingoville universe 'itself' (mainly the Mingoville School) that we shall explore in this paper.

As stated above the paratextual nature of hypertexted and digital material can be contested on the assumption that such paratexts provide a context for a homogeneous original 'main' text. As illustrated by Mingoville, online learning platforms cannot necessarily be described as coherent works with adherent paratexts that serve to introduce them. This becomes apparent in Mingoville as both the learning activities found in the two platform zones and the introductory first main web page consist of separate loosely interdependent items that do not necessarily come together in any consistent hierarchical order. However, as some of the platform items are defined as activities and some as guides or introductions, the platform does to some extent operate with the idea of a main and auxiliary texts. In addition to this, the main web page and the learning zones of Mingoville are separated by a login process which requires a license for the user to continue into the learning process. The main web page and the learning zones are therefore both separated and connected through introductory paratexts which shape and support the learner experience as well as creating interest in the commercial product. In this sense the function of the paratextual elements of Mingoville, specifically the teacher guide, is doubly performative as an advisory and introductory collection of textual and visual elements that also serve to celebrate and recommend the platform as a learning material. As stated in the teacher guide, Mingoville "offers virtual learning tools to help children learn English more effectively". The efficiency of Mingoville is, according to the teacher guide, based on the principles that children learn English best when there is an element of fun, when they are immersed in the language, and when there are a variety of methods of learning available, as not all children learn in the same way.

Figure 1: *Paratextual elements in the Mingoville platform*

On the one hand, the Mingoville platform contains a number of intertwined textual and visual elements that are not hierarchically ordered; on the other hand, an educational 'text' like Mingoville seems to need auxiliary texts such as teacher and parent guides, as its status as an educational material appears to necessitate some kind of instruction or instructional guidance. This seems even more relevant when the teaching material takes the form of a game, or game-based activities in which the pupil is often seen to be the primary actor or interpreter.

5. TEACHER ADDRESS AND TEACHER GUIDANCE IN MINGOVILLE

In Mingoville, the role of the teacher is primarily addressed in two para-textual elements of the platform, i.e. a teacher guide which can be down-loaded from the menu bar of the main web page and a teacher avatar, who introduces tasks and exercises to the learners in the Mingoville School zone. In addition to this, the Mingoville School platform zone offers the teacher planning, evaluation, and administration tools, which can give him or her an overview of platform tasks, and allows him or her to customise and modify missions, as well as define missions to be worked on by pupils. These teacher tools situate the teacher in an administrative, evaluative, and planning position with regard to e.g. individualising and customising instruction. In this paper we shall focus mainly on the teacher avatar and the teacher guide, as these paratextual elements situate the teacher respectively inside and outside the main activities of the learning platform (Mingoville School).

The teacher guide explains to the teacher how the platform has been designed, and which curriculum goals and skills can be addressed by the individual tasks. In the teacher guide the role of the teacher is therefore mainly understood as game external, i.e. as a role that involves knowledge of and an attention to curriculum aims and related pedagogy. In comparison, the role of the teacher avatar in the Mingoville School zone is game inter-nal, i.e. the Mingo teacher avatar acts as a substitute for the teacher within the individual tasks and games of the Mingoville School zone. Within the platform tasks the role of the teacher (represented by the Mingo avatar) is understood as mainly instructional, as the teacher avatar introduces tasks and gives feedback to the pupil.

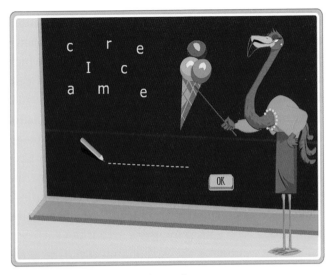

Figure 2: *The teacher avatar in Mingoville*

The role of the teacher in Mingoville is primarily connected to the Mingoville School zone as this is the platform zone that most visibly remediates the school activities of exercise, repetition, and practice. In the Mingoville Virtual World, by contrast, teacher intervention is not conceptualised as a visible aspect of platform interaction. This may be due to the fact that the Mingoville Virtual World focuses on playing rather than learning and that the activities in the Virtual World are designed for children to practise using English while having fun with interaction and games, while the Mingoville School Zone focuses on learning English to a greater extent as a goal of the activities (some of which are game-based). The focus on "play now" activities in the Mingoville Virtual World therefore seems to marginalise adult intervention and guidance, i.e. the teacher is not a visible presence in the virtual world, which is primarily student-directed. Intervention is however present in the form of safe chat, a function added by the company to restrict and control language and information exchange online.

6. TEACHER ADDRESS IN GLOBAL CONFLICTS

Global Conflicts is a role-playing adventure game set in a 3D environment in which the student plays a freelance journalist who has to explore particular issues or conflicts in, for instance, Latin America or the Middle

East – i.e. violation of human rights, corruption, pollution, immigration, etc. Thus the various versions of the games take place within different semiotic domains, which are understood as areas or sets of activities in which one thinks, acts, and assesses in a particular way (Gee 2007b). Within these semiotic domains, students are required to act as journalists affiliated with a newspaper. The game can be defined as an epistemic game (Shaffer 2006); it is the journalistic practice which comprises the game's focal point. When the students adopt the journalist avatar within the game, they have to undertake research and, using their findings, produce articles for the newspaper. This is done by "interviewing" different characters within a given a timeframe and collecting "counter-arguments", which must be used in a confrontational interview with responsible authorities such as a "factory owner" or a "mayor" waiting at the end of a mission. The game includes certain inbuilt dynamics such as a timeframe and a points system awarding points for arguments gathered.

Like Mingoville, Global Conflicts is a collage of paratextual elements, some of which are guides. Game play is licensed (not free) and is introduced through a main web page (The Global Conflicts Portal), which consists of an introductory description of the game and its learning aims and potentials as well as testimonies from users. The main web page also has a menu with introductory guides such as "Getting Started" and "Teaching Resources". A teacher guide for each game theme (e.g. Latin America, Child Soldiers, Sweatshops) can be downloaded from the teaching resources menu.

In Global Conflicts the role of the teacher is conceptualised as being central to the learning experience, but mainly game external. Conversely, game internal focus is primarily on the journalist, i.e. the learner's avatar, who is the main character of the game narrative. In the game, the pupil is understood to be a central actor, as the learning potential of the game is connected with the pupil's ability to participate actively in the conflict in question through gaming. In the teacher guide the role of the pupil (and her/his learning) is therefore seen as significantly associated with the situated and participatory learning connected with gaming. This view of gaming as a learning process is often found in game theory, i.e. that gaming is an immersive experience in which the learner learns by participating in a near-real world, or in a world where action and feedback are situated (Shaffer 2006, Gee 2007):

"The pupils will get a chance to actively participate in a conflict and deal with issues that usually seem inaccessible to them, and the virtual context prevents the course content from becoming mindless memorisation. The content becomes a part

SERIOUS GAMES IN EDUCATION

of the pupils' personal experience – they get to actually talk to child labourers, to the people who hire them, to the children's families and to the NGO worker, but above all they get a chance to actively influence the storyline. These personal experiences are very valuable to the teaching and learning processes that follow, since they let the pupils assess a range of problems that they have now acquired a practical attitude to and that suddenly concern them in a very different way."

(http://www.globalconflicts.eu/media/teachingmat/sgi_mo_teachermanual_en.pdf)

Whereas the role of the learner in Global Conflicts is seen as predominantly game internal and game immersed, the role of the teacher is, as mentioned above, primarily game external. The role of the teacher in the game is closely tied to the learning theory of the game design, which focuses on the pupil's in-game experience and on an experiential learning approach. This learning approach is conceptualised by the initial teacher guide as "the introduction of different teaching modes, which stress different styles of learning. Learning involves a progression through the different modes." The different modes are "active experimentation" and "reflective observation" which are performed and directed by the pupils and the teacher respectively. The experiential learning approach therefore stresses the interplay between in-game experience and reflection before and after the game experience and is conceptualised as a cycle, or a circular process.

As stated in the teacher guide, the game therefore cannot stand by itself but should be facilitated by the teacher, who will be able to provide the necessary reflection on the learning process and the themes of the game experience. In the process of playing, discussing, and reflecting the teacher should therefore (according to the Global Conflicts teacher guide) be responsible for providing an overview of the political and historical aspects of the conflict studied (before the game experience) as well as for debriefing and discussion (after the game experience). During game play, the teacher's main occupation should be coordinating the transition between lectures, game, and reflections.

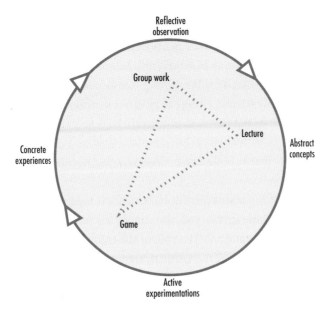

Figure 3: *Different approaches to learning in Global Conflicts, based on Kolb (1984).*

Global Conflicts is a game-based learning platform targeted at secondary school children who are not necessarily beginners in their subject, which may be one reason why it does not generally rely on in-game instruction and teacher intervention. In addition to this, Global Conflicts explicitly conceptualises learning as an interplay between exploratory in-game experience (initiated by the pupil) and pre- and post- game reflection (initiated by the teacher), which places the teacher outside the game, as a facilitator and discussant. Global Conflicts does indicate that the role of the teacher in the game-based learning experience is significant; however, the teacher is not conceptualised as a figure who is involved in the game experience itself, but rather as someone who provides the contextual knowledge and reflection to complete (or reiterate) the cycle of learning. This idea of learning extends the understanding of the game and therefore the game-based learning experience to reflection outside the world of the game itself.

7. CONCLUSION: THE TEACHER'S ROLE AND POSITIONS IN RELATION TO LEARNING GAMES

As argued above, the teacher's role is central in the use of digital learning tools and learning games as the teacher develops new teaching functions and new positions in relation to their students. Several studies have shown that often teachers do not actively teach when games are used in the process of learning, as they frequently rely on the students' activity and commitment levels. And these studies also demonstrate that the teacher's interventions are important for the students learning processes and outcomes (Egenfeldt-Nielsen 2007, Sørensen & Audon 2004).

Experiences from the Serious Games on a Global Market Place project's fieldwork have shown that the game-based learning tools discussed above are often introduced and applied without being placed within the broader context of the school subject, and without explicit subject-related goals for the activities. This may be due to the emergent status of game-based learning, which explains why digital games are not yet, and not easily, incorporated into practice. The emergent status of game-based learning in schools has therefore been a methodological problem in the project as research has often been based on experimental set-ups rather than the study of actual ongoing practice with learning games. The learning tools, as they have been understood and used by teachers in our research, have thus often been employed in singular lesson plans or for specific occasions, sometimes disconnected from other lessons. In the project, the Global Conflicts games were used by 19 different teachers from three countries (Denmark, Norway, and England). The majority of these teachers were first time users of Global Conflicts, a fact which underlines both the barriers to and possibilities for game-based learning. On the one hand, the teachers were interested in trying out a new learning tool, but on the other hand, as first time users, they were not very familiar with the game and often not competent enough to maintain usage (Hanghøj & Brund 2010).

A common feature in the use of these games has been that the teachers are largely situated backstage, and that they let the students play and explore the game on their own. In the studies of the Global Conflicts game the teachers were present and generally adopted a position as more or less curious observers, monitoring the students' activities on the screen. As such, they did not play a clear and active interventional role in their pupils' subject-related work with the games (ibid.). The Global Conflicts games, in terms of design, do not encourage teachers to participate actively in the game itself, i.e. as a player, as argued above. The design of the game therefore operates largely with students as players, and the game can in principle be played by students without any form of teacher intervention, even though the teacher guide suggests that the teacher frames and defines the learning process before, after, and, to some extent, during the game.

In our studies of Mingoville we have observed teachers leaving it up to the students themselves to work with the various elements of the game, as well as teachers who have made an effort to familiarise themselves with the game's activities and who have related Mingoville to a number of subject-relevant activities. With Mingoville, we have seen that teachers interpret the game both as an exploratory learning material, defined and played by the pupils, and as a learning material that needs teacher intervention and requires directed interaction. However, the direction and planning done by the teacher is often confined to game external activities, i.e. the game internal activity is mainly understood to be self-directed learning done by the pupil (alone or with peers). Many pupils see the platform in the same way, that is, they tend to skip the introductions given by the teacher avatar in Mingoville, and move on to the activity itself. Paratextual information such as that given by the Mingoville teacher avatar may thus be understood as superfluous information by a number of students; however, some pupils do need the instructions – and enjoy the feedback – of the teacher avatar. A closer study of the interaction of these pupils with Mingoville and the function of the teacher avatar in relation to the actual (present or absent) teacher will be an aspect of our further (and future) analysis of data. Judging from the experiences provided by the project concerning the roles and positions of the teacher when using learning games in school contexts, it is important that teachers are included in the construction of the educational design of the game to a greater extent than is currently the case. We have tried to conceptualise these approaches to the design of game-based learning through the concept of the paratext in order to understand how the teacher is actually addressed in the design and what this means for the ways in which the teacher can potentially participate in the game-based learning experience. When it comes to students and teachers, the main focus of the games has generally been on student activities.

REFERENCES:

Consalvo, M. 2007. *Cheating. Gaining advantage in Videogames.* MIT Press.
Egenfeldt-Nielsen, S. 2007. "Overview of research on the educational use of video games." In *Digital kompetense. Nordic Journal of Digital Literacy.* Oslo: Oslo University Press.
Gee, J. P. 2007. "Are Video Games Good for Learning?" In *Digital kompetense. Nordic Journal of Digital Literacy.* Oslo: Oslo University Press.

Genette, G. 1987. *Paratexts: thresholds of interpretation*. Literature, Culture, Theory 20. Cambridge: Cambridge University Press.

Hanghøj, T. & C. E. Brund. 2010. "Teacher Roles and Positionings in Relation to Educational Games." Paper presented at the 4th European Conference on Game-Based Learning, Danish School of Education, Aarhus University, October 21-22.

Kolb, D. A. 1984. *Experiential learning: Experience as the source of learning and development*. Englewood Cliffs: Prentice Hall.

Lunenfeld, P. 1999. *Unfinished business*. In *The digital dialectic*, edited by P. Lunenfeld. New Essays on New Media. MIT Press.

Shaffer, K. D. 2006. *How Computer Games Help Children Learn*. New York: Palgrave Macmillan.

Sørensen, B. H., L. Audon, & K. Levinsen. 2010. *Skole 2.0*. Aarhus: Klim.

5. GAME AND PLAY

5 A. LEARNING GAMES AND THE DISRUPTIVE EFFECTS OF PLAY

Carsten Jessen

1. INTRODUCTION

For more than 25 years scholars have had great expectations of computer games as an educational aid, but there is still a string of questions which need to be solved, not least concerning the balance between the game as motivation and the desired learning outcome. Most current scholars seem to agree that video games are an untapped resource in the field of education and that this is partly due to bad game design and partly to teachers with a lack of knowledge about games (Pivec & Pivec 2008, Ulicsak 2010). This is undoubtedly a substantial part of the explanation for the slow acceptance of game-based learning. Nevertheless, in this article I will argue that the problem is not wholly constituted by either games or teachers, or a combination of the two; instead, it is the phenomenon of *play* that disrupts the interplay between games and learning, which, in a pedagogical context, is expected to be a productive combination.

2. INTERDISCIPLINARITY, HAMMERS AND NAILS

The difficulty with games in education may very well be that, as a research field, it is interdisciplinary; education and gamesare separate academic disciplines. Every research area has a tendency to interpret its surroundings via its fundamental theories, which carry certain perspectives or even a worldview that unavoidably colour observations, and it is often almost impossible to work across disciplines without causing a discussion about who has the right to define the identity of research objects. To put it bluntly, in the words of the psychologist Maslow: "If you only have a hammer, you tend to see every problem as a nail." Research areas have difficulty in acknowledging their own limitations. Nevertheless, one is often forced to recognise such limitations in order to prevent all nearby phenomena from becoming "nails".

Paraphrasing the excerpt from Maslow, one might say that "to all educational researchers, every human activity is connected to learning", without really provoking anyone within the pedagogical field, because it is a fact that learning is present everywhere: it would be just as uncontroversial as arguing that the human is based on biology. Both these statements are correct, but there is of course a catch. For instance, there is a difference between arguing that the human consists of biology, on the one hand, and viewing all human actions from the point of view of biology. From a biological point of view, all human actions risk being interpreted via theories about the species' struggle for survival, which is rarely a suitable outset for understanding and describing cultural phenomena. Similarly, seeing all human activities as constituting learning is a result of one specific viewpoint. It is important to uphold a clear distinction between learning and the activities in question, because clearly *the fact* that one learns something does not entail that the given activity was *meant* to ensure learning.

When computer games are employed as an object in pedagogical practice and research, it is only natural that the game is viewed from the perspective of learning. Obviously, it is legitimate and relevant to try to understand how games can be used for learning purposes, but there is a definite risk that games become "nails" in the pedagogical frame of reference. In fact, the term "risk" is too vague, because it began to happen long ago. In the first serious academic studies of computer games in the early 1980s, the main focus was the importance of games for learning and education (Malone 1981, Loftus and Loftus 1984, Greenfield 1984). This in itself does not necessarily pose a problem, especially not today when game research has been established as an independent research area in which pedagogical research does not play a key role. The problem arises when educational game studies do not realise or acknowledge its limitations with regard to games that arise because, like many other phenomena, games were not originally invented with the purpose of generating learning. They may be useful as a means for education and learning. Indeed, it is plausible, considering the host of positively loaded publications that appear in international academic literature on the subject these days; and in this context it may, of course, be interesting to ask if it really matters whether games were originally meant to be one thing or the other. If games are able to deliver the goods in the form of the desired learning outcomes, then what is the problem? The answer is that there is still no evidence that games can be used uncomplicatedly for educational purposes and targeted learning. Things do take time, but 25 years is a long time, and it is quite likely that there *is* a problem. As mentioned above, the problem may be the phenomenon of *play*, or, rather, the *interpretation* of play from an educational perspective.

3. GAMES GENERATE LEARNING

Let us begin the discussion on games and learning vs. play by demonstrating the obvious fact that games generate learning. Empirically, it is easy to demonstrate. A simple test of this statement can be conducted by giving a child of just about any age a new, unknown game, letting the child play the way it wants to for a week or two, and evaluating the results. If the game appealed to the child, it is very likely that it has learned to play the game. As computer games research has often pointed out, this is not only true for simple games, but also for relatively complicated games that require significant knowledge and a considerable working effort, including planning and strategies (e.g. Loftus and Loftus 1984, Greenfield 1984, Jessen 1999a, Jessen 2002, Gee 2003, Shaffer 2006, Gee 2007, Thomas & Seely Brown 2011). So: games do generate learning, and since they are also highly motivating, the idea of using games as learning material seems rather obvious.

One can approach this idea from various directions. Developing games which, as opposed to most commercial games, have a learning objective of an academic character – in other words, producing serious games – is the obvious choice. Several attempts have been made to do precisely this, among other places in the so-called "edutainment" genre which, in brief, is defined as "a form of entertainment (as by games, films, or shows) that is designed to be educational" (Konzack 2000). So far, edutainment is the most widely distributed genre, with the most games on the educational market. Basically, the idea behind this type of game is simply to utilise games' motivating qualities to facilitate learning. The assumption is that it is possible to maintain the games' entertaining formal features while loading them with academic content. To date, the results from this idea have been somewhat insubstantial. Either the games fail to bring about the desired learning outcome or they fail to motivate the players sufficiently. A part of the reason for this can probably be found in the fact that most games are built on a simplified utilisation of behaviouristic learning theories which most modern educational research has abandoned. Gradually, negative associations have attached themselves to the concept of edutainment, and instead the new topic of interest is "serious games". The naïve belief that entertainment and learning can be united without problems has been abandoned, although there is a recurring belief that games and learning can be combined. Several new reports on games and learning state that uniting games and targeted learning is not an uncomplicated process (Pivec & Pivec 2008, Perlin, Plass, & Stratton 2010, Ulicsak 2010). Though there is still not much evidence to support their learning effects, games can have success in education, as long as the choice of game, the situated environment, and the teacher's role are considered carefully. Research on the subject is still in an early phase, confronting a number of unsolved theoretical as well as practical problems, with no definitive knowledge of how games can be integrated into teaching practices. Using games as learning material may be an obvious idea, but it is not easy to implement.

4. INFORMAL LEARNING VIA COMPUTERS

The idea of using computer games for teaching and learning can be approach from the opposite direction, that is, by analysing *how* one learns when playing computer games. For instance, children learn surprisingly quickly when playing commercial games; they often learn surprisingly complicated material and, they clearly do not learn in the same way that they do from traditional teaching forms. This has puzzled many scientists, who have used this as a starting point for studies in the form of learning that occurs in front of and via computers. Greenfield (1984) is one of the pioneers in this area, and in the early 1980s she discovered what has later been known as children's informal learning via computers. Her work still merits attention today:

> *Perhaps the most interesting part of video games as complex systems is the fact that the rules of the game are not given in advance. One must figure out the rules via observation, the trial and error method and via a process of testing hypotheses. [...] This process, which consists of observing, formulating hypotheses and working out the rules via a trial and error process, is basically the cognitive process of inductive discovery. By way of this process, we learn something about the world, and, at a more formal level, it is the process of thought that lies beneath scientific thinking and discovery.* (Greenfield 1984, 17, 19)

This thoroughly constructivist view of computer games remains highly relevant today, seeing as computer games are now far more complex and widespread and, therefore, far more practicable vis-à-vis learning than the relatively simple games Greenfield once observed. Nevertheless, it was not until the turn of the millennium that studies of learning processes in connection with computer games really began to pick up speed in several research groups with different points of departure. In Denmark this was most obvious in connection with a research project on the changing face of childhood culture and digital media that was carried out in the period from 1997 to 2002 (Sørensen 2002a), discussing and developing concepts such as formal and informal learning and learning networks, using children's play centred around the computer as its starting point. Part of this research focused specifically on the considerable and inescapable significance of one child to another when they learn to master complicated online games (Jessen 2002). At the same time and in a form that was much more focused on the development of games for learning, the learning processes connected with computer games were described by Gee (2003), in his expressively-titled book *What computer games can teach us about learning*. In addition, Shaffer (2006) with his so-called "epistemic games", in which the professional practices of, for instance, a research journalist or an urban planner are transferred to learning games, is responsible for a widespread use of this type of game. In a way, Shaffer's idea is a more developed and nuanced version of what Seymour Papert (1980) termed "Microworlds". In brief, the research mentioned here demonstrated the constructivist thought represented by Greenfield. On this basis, games for learning can be thought of and developed as demarcated universes that stimulate a form of social practice in which the players can act and learn the "rules" of this practice. This way of thinking about computer games has been developed even further lately by Thomas and Seely Brown (2011), who argue that online games like *World of Warcraft* represent a new learning culture that can and ought to inspire education in the 21st century, mainly because games can teach us to cope with ongoing change in our current society. Thomas and Seely Brown, like Gee (2003) and Jessen (2002), expand their research into the communities surrounding online games and point out that these "cultures" can be explained using Lave and Wenger's (1991) theories about situated learning in social communities.

Considering the work of the abovementioned scholars, it may be established that players do learn something from games, even if it is difficult to target this learning accurately. But, there are other problems with this approach to games and learning besides accurate targeting. First and foremost, it is difficult to balance the motivation of the game and the desired learning outcome. Games that are created for education are often not particularly motivating compared with commercial games that have no specific learning goals (Pivec & Pivec 2008). On the other hand, the learning generated from commercial games is not considered academically acceptable in the traditional sense (Thomas and Seely Brown 2011). Motivation is of less vital importance, though, when games are used in schools, where voluntariness is not a central factor. However, if students consider playing a *duty*, the original number one cause for introducing games into education, the motivational power disappears, and then what is left of the argument for using games in an educational context? Thus, a high degree of motivation should perhaps not be the main argument for educational games. We will pursue this question in the following.

5. GAMES AND GAMES RESEARCH

There is a third approach to the idea that games generate learning. One might contemplate games in their original sense: not material for learning, but a phenomenon with a significance of its own. From this point of view the question is not how games can be used in an educational context, but what games are as an independent cultural phenomenon. It would be natural to ask this question before even beginning to develop learning games, because it seems self-evident that knowledge about what it is about games that appeals to players is of considerable value. Nevertheless, a large part of the games industry and research into learning games have been satisfied with concluding that games are tempting and motivating without really contemplating why this is the case.

Approaching the relatively new academic branch of "game studies", which deals with games as cultural phenomena and computer games in particular, one must conclude that so far research has not arrived at an altogether clear and unequivocal result. There is a multitude of perspectives on games, which is only to be expected from a new science. In general, game researchers are interested in games in the same way that literary studies are interested in literature and film studies in film. Today, a significant part of game studies is well on its way to becoming a normalised academic discipline with a similar tradition for developing tools for analysis, definition attempts, and discussions of how games are different from aesthetic media such as literature and film, and what else is part of an aesthetic academic context. Jesper Juul contributes with one of the most unambiguous, yet widespread, definitions of what constitutes a game:

> *A game is a rule-based system with a variable and quantifiable outcome, where different outcomes are assigned different values, the player exerts effort in order to influence the outcome, the player feels emotionally attached to the outcome, and the consequences of the activity are optional and negotiable.* (Juul 2005, 36)

Unfortunately, no matter how precise the definition, the facts that games are rule-based systems to which the player must be emotionally attached and that a result is needed do not bring us much closer to our answer. The formal characteristics of games do not tell us much about what motivates their players.

Nevertheless, one need not search for long in game studies before it becomes evident that *play*, according to most researchers, is an important factor. Prominent play scholars like Johan Huizinga, Roger Callois, and Brian Sutton-Smith appear in numerous articles and books on the topic. For instance, Jesper Juul's definition of games above draws on all three (Juul 2005, 30). If anything, play is the most important factor in what can be referred to as the standard work on games today: Salen and Zimmerman's *Rules of Play* (2004). In this book, which is about designing games as well as game theory, the authors identify a connection between games and play. They define the goal of successful game design as "the creation of meaningful play" and later on state that "Rules are merely the means for creating play" (Salen and Zimmerman 2004, 33, 302). And to make the central point absolutely clear, they argue in a subsequent anthology on games that "Games create play: of that there is no doubt" (Salen and Zimmerman 2006, 83). In other words, games fulfil a function in relation to play. They can be seen as means or tools that generate play (Jessen 1999b, Jessen & Karoff 2008). From this point of view, Juul's fairly formal definition of games makes sense. It captures how games must be designed in order to generate play.

Whether anything new has been said on the subject of games and learning by pointing out that games create play depends, naturally, on the definition of play. In developmental psychology, play is primarily a means for learning (Piaget 1972, Vygotsky 1967, Singer, Golinkoff, & Hirsh-Pasek 2006) and, in that frame of reference, it follows logically from the statement that games generate play that they also generate learning. To game studies it is not that simple, with good reason. Based on the work of the abovementioned play scholars, play is, in and by itself, a meaningful human activity that we practise for the simple joy of it (now is the time to remember Maslow's saying about hammers and nails). If play is an end point in itself and not simply a means, it may explain the problem with the assumption that games can motivate learning.

6. PLAY AND PLAY RESEARCH

The work of Brian Sutton-Smith, who, on the basis of 50 years of research into the topic in question, is the most highly esteemed play researcher, is a good outset for examining play. In his latest book, *The Ambiguity of Play*, he makes a supreme effort, unparalleled in play research, to provide an overview of the concept of play. He takes as his starting point the notion that play is a scientifically ambiguous concept that has never been satisfactorily defined, and certainly not unambiguously so. Instead, a series of different theories on play exist which do not correspond. Sutton-Smith chooses to categorise these many theories into what he calls "seven rhetorics of play". Each of these seven rhetorics or discourses comprise a view of what play is and what its function is. The first and most well-known is "the rhetoric of play as progress" which describes the function of play as a means for development, learning, and adaptation and is defended within educational studies and developmental psychology, as well as biology. This conception is not absolute in science; it is accompanied by other discourses, such as "the rhetoric of play as the imaginary" and "the rhetoric of play as identity", among others. Reading Sutton-Smith's book, it may seem as if the seven discourses are presented as more or less equal hypotheses on play, each focusing on different aspects of play which are of interest to different academic fields. In these cases as well as in numerous others, play seems to have potential as "raw material" that can be shaped and used in various contexts. Such an approach to play can more or less be sustained until the seventh and last discourse is introduced, "the rhetoric of play as frivolous", which describes play as frivolous, silly, giddy, foolish, shallow, insignificant, and unimportant. Here, Sutton-Smith places the seven discourses within one collective perspective that regards the discourse on play as "frivolous" as an underlying theme in all the other discourses. They all relate to this discourse by distinguishing between useful and useless play in different ways. According to Sutton-Smith.

> It can be ventured that the denigration of frivolous play actually subdivides itself into six different kinds of devalued play, each of which, in its own way, helps to sustain the six types of play that are lauded by these rhetorics (Sutton-Smith 1997, 204)

In the other six discourses, the discourse on play as frivolous is marginalised, as "wrong" play, which, according to Sutton-Smith, is a central dimension of our historical understanding of play. He refers to "the fight that have taken place, since ancient Greek society, between the Apollonian views of play as rational and the Dionysian view of play as irrational" (Sutton-Smith 1997, 204). He sees the other six discourses as attempts to exercise cultural hegemony over frivolous play.

> What is important is that the games of the less powerful groups are implicitly excluded or even ridiculed. [...] Those who have lauded the imaginary kind of play are the social and intellectual elites, always concerned to differentiate their own sophisticated social or solitary playfulness from that of the masses. (Sutton-Smith 1997, 205)

Sutton-Smith does not suggest that "the rhetoric of play as frivolous" is a better description of play than the others; it is not merely another discourse that is comparable with the other six. Instead, it represents a constant and disturbing aspect in the attempts to define play.

7. A THEORY OF PLAY AND GAMES

Of course, the main question is whether a discourse of play as frivolous can be used to qualify an understanding of what play, as an independent phenomenon, is. Again, it is useful to turn to Brian Sutton-Smith in his capacity both as a play researcher and a child researcher. Several years ago, in a short article, he presented one of the most precise definitions of play to date:

> [...] we postulate as the aboriginal paradigm for play, mother and infant conjoined in an expressive communicational frame within which they contrastively participate in the modulation of excitement. We call this a paradigm for all ludic action, because we suggest that other play itself is a metaphoric statement of this literal state of affairs. Ludic action, wherever it is, always involves the analogous establishment of the secure communicational frame and the manipulation of excitement arousal through contrastive actions within that frame. (Sutton-Smith 1979, 300-301)

This description of the interplay between mother and child as archetypal play is characterised by encompassing the central features within play theories that do not regard play as mainly useful in regard to learning or development; this includes the theories of Johan Huizinga, Gregory Bateson, Roger Caillois, and H. G. Gadamer. Sutton-Smith's definition is also characterised by its basis in empirical research which, at the time in question, was revolutionary because it employed a novel research methodology that enabled observations of a yet unseen degree of precision, namely via video recordings. Sutton-Smith developed this definition from the psychologist Daniel Stern's ground-breaking studies of the interplay between mother and infant (Stern 1977) that showed that the part played by the infant is highly active, and not that of the passive recipient previously described by developmental psychology.

"Modulation of excitement" is a very precise description of what we do when we play; at the same time, it comprises a precise description of what play is, that is to say, a particularly intense atmosphere. Furthermore, the description clarifies the idea that play is generated via the players' focused and conscious actions. In other words, Sutton-Smith thus emphasises that acts of play are also *reflective actions*. The players, including infants, relate to their own actions and those of others and control them (socially or individually) for the purpose of creating a specific state, the "state of play", of which there are numerous variations. For instance, play can be physical, making the body move forwards and backwards, as in sports, dancing, or on a swing; it might be psychological, creating and using a mental tension, for which jokes or horror stories are good examples. It is remarkable in this context that we often generate play by directly using the natural reactions of the body and mind, such as dizziness or fear.

We employ countless forms of tools, techniques, or genres of physical as well as immaterial types to help initiate activities that make us play. Thus, games are just one out of numerous tools (Jessen 1999b, Salen and Zimmerman 2004, Rodriguez 2006, Jessen & Karoff 2008), but in order to understand games it is important to emphasise that they are cultural products which have been formed as tools via a long history. In other words, they are tools that have been shaped so as to perform a specific task, much like a hammer.

8. CONSEQUENCES FOR LEARNING GAMES

From the perspective outlined above, games are suitable for generating play, but not necessarily for generating purposive learning. Therefore, making games a tool for learning is not a simple operation that merely involves modifying existing game forms and genres. Most research and practice concerning learning games do not recognise games and play as independent phenomena. This leaves blind spots, for instance, when trying to understand why one is unable to achieve an expected learning result. There is indeed a problem if one assumes that the game's act of play in itself can facilitate learning. The opposite is often the case, either in the form of boredom, because the learning game fails to generate the state of play that the players expect, or because frivolous play infiltrates the act and takes over the situation.

The consequence of the above interpretation of games might be the recognition that one's focus while creating learning games should not simply be on generating play and fun; instead, one should distinguish between games for the purpose of learning and games for the purpose of play. Games can be engaging, perhaps even exciting and fun, even if their purpose is not a state of play.[1] The underlying basis of learning games should be that we are faced with a new and different evolving genre. At the moment, the field's most promising research is trying to use digital technology as the basis for independent interactive universes, controlled by rules, which can be seen as a form of "materialisation" of theoretical models with which the users can interact almost on a par with natural laws, like Patricia Greenfield's description written nearly 25 years ago. In relation to learning games, the most interesting thing about digital technology is the fact that there are virtually no limitations to how the rules of "micro universes" can be formed, so that abstract models, which do not lend themselves easily to clear communication and classroom teaching, are accessible in interactive form. Digital games are not only rule-based systems. They are first and foremost *digital*. When playing traditional non-digital games, rules have to be learned in advance and strictly obeyed before you are able to play. In contrast, rules are manifest when playing digital games, which means they can be observed via inductive discovery. The players can figure out the rules via manipulation and experimentation, that is, via a trial and error process, which is fundamental to learning. Furthermore, and this is of central importance to learning games, these manifest rules can be shaped in nearly any direction into what I would like to term "intelligent material". In fact, nearly any digital game can be used as an example of such material, but complex games like the strategy games *Simcity*, *Roller Coaster Tycoon*, and *Civilization* are brilliant illustrations. If such games are combined with an online community, which is the case with online games today, the result is the kind of learning com-

---

1   For some types of games, play can have a distinct purpose of its own; for example, when the clear aim is to create physical play in order to fight obesity, which is the case with digital playgrounds (Lund, Klitbo, & Jessen 2005).

munity that Thomas and Seely Brown find a "nearly perfect illustration" of a new learning culture of the 21st century. In this sense, digital games can be viewed as educational innovations with novel didactic potentials, but also with novel demands as regards didactic design. Precisely with regard to design, it is unhelpful to assume that the motivation from games aimed at play can be easily transferred to learning games, because the fact is that by focusing too much on play as a motivating force learning potentials are easily overlooked. The last part of this article will contemplate this problem in more detail.

As mentioned above, it is easy to conclude that games lead to learning and that computer games and learning are especially closely connected, because such games are often complicated. However, the relation between games and learning is the opposite of the one needed for learning games in education. One does not play computer games in order to learn. Quite the reverse: the players learn in order to keep playing and in order to play with others (Jessen 2002, Sørensen 2006, Arnseth 2006). In the case of computer games, the players engage in every learning process on account of the wish that sooner or later it will lead to the above described state of play.

From the perspective of learning, it is not the game itself that is interesting, but its learning potential. If one approaches this differently, steers clear of the game and the motivation, and instead asks how the players learn when they play, new perspectives with regard to the design of learning games appear. James Paul Gee (2003) pointed out long ago that commercial computer games contain acute knowledge about learning processes, even if their purpose is not learning. This knowledge is not theoretically well-defined, but on the other hand it has been tested in practice within a tough business by millions of players, because commercial games depend on the players' ability to quickly and efficiently learn how to act in games that demand that the players acquire comprehensive new knowledge.

Gee demonstrates that analyses of both games and the players' practice can produce valuable knowledge on the subject of learning. However, these analyses challenge the educational-didactic way of thought, because computer games employ learning forms other than those of teaching in general. The players do not learn in the same way that they do in classrooms (Gee 2003, Ito et al. 2008). Briefly and simplified outlined, one can say that in conventional didactic thinking, academic knowledge is often presented in a step by step format of which the starting point is fundamental knowledge that is gradually made more and more complex. In this carefully designed progressive development, every new step builds on the previous one. Countless teaching aids are designed for this form of teaching.

This kind of didactic approach has proven difficult to transfer to the informal learning contexts of computer games, because it presupposes constant control on the part of the teacher, and because motivation is often an external factor in connection with academic knowledge, that is to say, grades and assessments, not needs or interests, are the motivating elements. The fundamental problem with edutainment games is precisely the difficulties involved in understanding motivation as distinct from needs; this type of game demonstrates that step by step thinking, which may work in the classroom, is not particularly well-suited as a basis for the design of learning games.

In computer games, the motivation for learning is the players' distinct need for knowledge. The acquisition of new knowledge and new skills is a prerequisite for playing, and in most games the acquisition of additional knowledge remains a prerequisite throughout. At the same time, the players are keenly aware that the new knowledge and skills that must be acquired, sometimes with much difficulty, are significant and useful. Therefore, a game must be designed in such a way that the player is able to recognise the importance and function of each knowledge component and skill for his or her chance to keep playing.

The impact of the above facts on game design becomes even more obvious if we consider the players' practice, in which the social aspect plays a central role; this is especially clear in online role-playing. The acquisition of knowledge is a central focus point for social relations in this type of game (Jessen 2002, Thomas and Seely Brown 2011). Being in possession of knowledge and skills is the foundation for each player's social status, which is crucial for forming groups that are strong enough to solve problems in the game, for instance, to win battles in an online game like *World of Warcraft*, which demands collaboration between highly skilled players. Thus, it is important for each player to continue acquiring new knowledge and to improve one's skills. Seeing as the players are thus dependent on other players' knowledge, especially as beginners, the participants' status and identity not only manifest themselves in their actual performance in battle, but also to a significant degree in the exchange of knowledge in the community's social practice, in which the ability of the more experienced to pass knowledge on to the less experienced establishes his or her social status. The fact that the players' level is clearly marked in the games demonstrates the importance of this aspect in online communities. All players are on a specific level and constantly on their way to the next. In the communities surrounding the games it is common practice to congratulate a player who moves to another level.

What can this brief example tells us about the design of learning games? In connection with the above, it is tempting once more to focus on motivation, not in the form of play this time, but in the form of social status, which is unquestionably easier to deal with as a motivating factor in learning contexts than frivolous play. Paradoxically, this example also demonstrates that acknowledging game and play as independent cultural phenomena enables one to view the learning processes more clearly. When one is not hypnotised by the motivational power of games, it becomes possible to analyse the learning forms that they make possible, and in the above example it is obvious that learning in online games is, to a great extent, based on whether the players have a well-functioning *learning community* and an accessible *learning network* consisting of more experienced players. These communities and networks contain important learning potentials that are not exclusive to games. They can both be found around other computer games (Jessen 1999a) and around other digital media (Sørensen 2002a, Sørensen 2005) as well as in many activities undertaken by children, young people, and adults (Wenger 1997). They are so common that one is inclined to agree with James Paul Gee when he argues, on the subject of the purpose of analysing learning in connection with computer games, that "What we are really looking for here is this: the theory of human learning built into good video games" (Gee 2003, 6).

Learning communities and learning networks are not the only important aspects as regards learning in relation to games, but they are central elements and, thus, good examples of what must be considered in the design of learning games, including the importance of social aspects. Above all, they suggest that the design of good learning games might depend on how specialist knowledge is structured. In order for a learning game to work in and make use of the potentials of the learning community and learning network, the learning aids must be structured in such a way that knowledge can be *exchanged socially* which, among other things, entails that it should not be given in advance; instead, the acquisition of knowledge should depend on the participants' work effort, so that knowledge in itself is of value in the community.

REFERENCES

Anchor, R. 1978. "History and Play: Johan Huizinga and His Critics." *History and Theory* (17)1.

Arnseth, H. C. 2006. "Learning to Play or Playing to Learn – A Critical Account of the Models of Communication Informing Educational Research on Computer Gameplay." *Game Studies* (6)1.

Bateson, G. 1956. "The message 'This is play.'" In *Group processes: Transactions of the second conference*, edited by B. Schaffner. New York: Josiah Macy, Jr. Foundation.

Buhl, M., B. H. Sørensen, & B. Meyer, eds. 2006. *Media and ICT – learning potentials*. Copenhagen: Danish University of Education Press. Available at http://www.dpu.dk/site.aspx?p=8803, accessed on 03.11.11

Callois, R. 1961. *Man, Play and Games*. New York: The Free Press of Glencoe.

Egenfeldt-Nielsen, S. 2006. "Overview of research on educational use of video games." *Digital kompetense*. 1(3).

Egenfeldt-Nielsen, S. 2005 *Beyond Edutainment: Exploring the Educational Potential of Computer Games*. Copenhagen: IT-University Copenhagen.

Gee, J. P. 2003. *What Video Games Have to Teach Us about Learning and Literacy*. New York: Palgrave Macmillan.

Gee, J. P. 2007. *Good video games + good learning. Collected essays on video games, learning, and literacy*. New York: Peter Lang.

Greenfield, P. 1984. *Mind and Media: The effects of television, Video games and Computers*. Cambridge Mass: Harvard University Press.

Huizinga, J. 2006. *Homo Ludens*. Boston: Beacon Press.

Ito, M., H. A. Horst, M. Bittanti, D. Boyd, B. Herr-Stephenson, P. T. Lange, C. J. Pascoe, & L. Robinson. 2008. *Living and Learning with New Media: Summary of Findings from the Digital Youth Project*. The John D. and Catherine T. MacArthur Foundation Reports on Digital Media and Learning.

Jessen, C. 1999a. *Children's Computer Culture. Three essays on Children and Computers*. Working Paper 8. Child and Youth Culture. Odense: Odense University.

Jessen, C. 1999b. *Computer games and play culture – an outline of an interpretative framework*. Originally published in Danish in *Børn, unge og medier*, edited by Christa Lykke Christensen. Gothenberg: Nordicom. Available at http://www.carsten-jessen.dk/compgames.html.

Jessen, C. 2002. "Virtual Communities as Learning Environment." In *Chatting. Play, Identity, Sociality and Learning*, edited by B. H. Sørensen. Research programme Media and ICT in a Learning Perspective. The Danish University of Education. Available at http://www.dpu.dk/fileadmin/www.dpu.dk/forskning/forskningsprogrammer/medierogitilaeringsperspektiv/publikationer/051221150158-amp-type-doc.

Jessen, C. & H. Karoff. 2008. "New play culture and playware." In *Det æstetiskes betydning i børns hverdagspraksis*, edited by Beth Juncker. BIN Norden. Available at http://bin-norden.ucsyd.dk/?download=3BINjessenkaroff.pdf.

Juul, J. 2005. *Half-real: Video Games between Real Rules and Fictional Worlds.* Cambridge: MIT Press.

Kahne, J., E. Middaugh, & C. Evans. 2008. *The Civic Potential of Video Games.* White paper. The John D. and Catherine T. MacArthur Foundation. Available at http://www.civicsurvey.org/White_paper_link_text.pdf.

Konzack, L. 2000. *Seriøse spil: Computerspil ej blot til lyst.* Available at http://design.emu.dk/artik/00/40-edutainment.html.

Konzack, L. 2003. *Edutainment – leg og lær med computermediet.* Aalborg: Aalborg University Press.

Lave, J. & E. Wenger. 1991. *Situated learning: legitimate peripheral participation.* Cambridge: Cambridge University Press.

Loftus, G. R. & E. F. Loftus. 1983. *Mind at Play. The Psychology of Video Games.* New York: Basic Books.

Lund, H.H., T. Klitbo, & C. Jessen. 2005. "Playware Technology for Physically Activating Play." *Artificial life and Robotics Journal* 9.

Magnussen, R. 2005. "Learning Games as a Platform for Simulated Science Practice." Paper presented at the *DIGRA Conference.* Vancouver, june 16-20 2005.

Magnussen, R. 2007. "Games as a Platform for Situated Science Practice." In *Worlds in Play: International Perspectives on Digital Games Research*, edited by Suzanne de Castell & Jennifer Jenson. New York: Peter Lang, 301-311.

Malone, T.W. 1981. "What makes computer games fun?" *BYTE* December 1981, 6: 258-277.

Malone, T. W. & M. R. Lepper. 1987. "Making learning fun: A taxonomy of intrinsic motivations for learning." In *Aptitude, Learning and Instruction*, edited by R. E. Snow and M. J. Farr. Vol. 3. Hillsdale, NJ: Erlbaum.

Papert, S. 1980. *Mindstorms.* New York: Basic Books.

Perlin, K., J. L. Plass, & S. Stratton. 2010. *Games for Learning.* Games for Learning Institute. Available at http://g4li.nyu.edu/May28_2010/report/forReviewByAttendees_May28_2010G4LI_Report.pdf, accessed on November 03 2011.

Piaget, J. 1972. *Play, Dreams and Imitation in Childhood.* London: Routledge and Kegan Paul.

Pivec, P. & M. Pivec. 2008. *Games in Schools.* Commissioned report for Interactive Software Federation of Europe (ISFE) by the European Commission (EC).

Research programme Media and ICT in a Learning Perspective. Copenhagen. The Danish University of Education. Available at http://www.dpu.dk/fileadmin/www.dpu.dk/forskning/forskningsprogrammer/medierogitilaeringsperspektiv/publikationer/051221150158-amp-type-doc, accessed on 03.11.11.

Rodriguez, H. 2006. "The Playful and the Serious: An approximation to Huizinga's Homo Ludens." *Games Studies* 6(2).

Salen, K. & E. Zimmerman. 2004. *Rules of play: game design fundamentals.* Cambridge, Mass.: MIT Press.

Salen, K. & E. Zimmerman. 2006. *The Game design reader: a rules of play anthology.* Cambridge, Mass.: MIT Press.

Shaffer, D. W. 2006. *How Computer Games Help Children Learn*. New York: Palgrave Macmillan.

Singer, D., R. M. Golinkoff, & K. Hirsh-Pasek, eds. 2006. *Play=Learning: How play motivates and enhances children's cognitive and social-emotional growth*. New York: Oxford University Press.

Stern, D. 1977. *The First Relationship: Infant and Mother*. Cambridge, Mass.: Harvard University Press.

Sutton-Smith, B. 1979. "Epilogue: Play as performance." In *Play and Learning*, edited by B. Sutton-Smith. New York: Gardner Press.

Sutton-Smith, B. 1997. *The Ambiguity of Play*. Cambridge, Mass.: Harvard University Press.

Sørensen, B. H., ed. 2002a. *Chatting. Play, Identity, Sociality and Learning*.

Sørensen, B. H. 2005. "ICT and the Gap Between School Pedagogy and Children's Culture." *Pedagogy, Culture and Society* 13(1).

Sørensen, B. H. 2006. "Digital Media and New Organisational Forms: Educational Knowledge Leadership." In. *Media and ICT: Learning Potentials*, edited by M. Buhl, B. Meyer, & B. H. Sørensen. Copenhagen: Danish School of Education Press.

Thomas, D. & J. Seely Brown. 2011. *A New Culture of Learning: Cultivating the Imagination for a World of Constant Change*. CreateSpace 2011.

Vygotsky, L. 1967. "Play and its role in the Mental Development of the Child." *Journal of Russian and East European Psychology*. Available at http://www.marxists.org/archive/vygotsky/works/1933/play.htm.

Ulicsak, M. 2010. *Games in Education: Serious Games*. Futurelab.

5 B. A GAME MAGICALLY CIRCLING

Stine Ejsing-Duun

This chapter analyses the relationship between players, the game world, and the ordinary world in alternative reality games (ARGs) and location-based games (LBGs). These games use technology to create a game world in the everyday scene. The topic of this chapter is the concept of the 'magic circle', which defines the relationship between play and the ordinary world, and how this concept relates to a new kind of game.

The games that are magically circling in this chapter are ARGs and LBGs. An ARG can be defined as a game that is based on a narrative that is explored and partly created by players. The players have to detect, examine, and explore possible clues that can help them advance in the game (and the story). One of the challenges is to decide if a message is actually part of the game (world) or not – and to find out what it signifies. This is made possible through collaboration between the players. An ARG is a game that 'refuses' to be a game: it frames itself as being part of ordinary life rather than being play. ARGs frequently involve a number of different media such as mobile phones, web, mail, e-mail, actors, radio, etc. LBGs are also games that are played on the boundary between play and ordinary world; however, the defining feature of LBGs is that the locations of the players in physical space affects the outcome of the game. This means that LBGs are situated on the boundary between play and ordinary life, using a combination of physical and digital media. Whilst ARGS are played entirely online, players of LBGs have to venture out into streets or parks.

In this chapter it is argued that when a game is placed in the everyday scene it is not possible to uphold a magic circle, and we therefore need another understanding of the limits between the ordinary world and the game world when playing ARGs or LBGs. To develop this understanding the chapter draws upon Michael Apter's theory about motivation and play, in which the focus is on the players' approach to the game instead of strict rules that sustain the magic circle as presented by Huizinga (1993) and Salen and Zimmerman (2004). Apter's view makes it possible to integrate the ordinary world and the game world without losing the magic of the game.

According to this author's definition of LBGs, they:

> *make it possible for players to act out, express relations at, or appropriate locations using digital and physical media; between multiple frames of ordinary life and play; and within fictional and authentic structures.* (Ejsing-Duun 2011)

LBGs are a part of ordinary life, as they are played on the boundary between play and the ordinary world. Although they do not involve physical locations, ARGs also play with frames of reference. The game researcher Jane McGonigal uses the term *immersive games* to describe ARGs; according to her, they are a subset of pervasive play which

> *[...] consists of "mixed reality" games that use mobile, ubiquitous and embedded digital technologies to create virtual playing fields in everyday spaces. Immersive games [...] are a form of pervasive play distinguished by the added element of their (somewhat infamous) "This is not a game" rhetoric.*(McGonigal 2003, 1-2)

According to McGonigal, ARGs thus do not separate themselves from the everyday space but deliberately try to erase the boundaries between the game and reality (ibid.). There is a mismatch between this and the idea of the 'magic circle', as proposed by the Dutch culture historian Johan Huizinga (Huizinga 1993), which has been developed and related to games by Salen and Zimmerman (2004). The aim of this chapter is to show how players of different types of ARGs are in fact *not leaving the ordinary world* to enter a magical circle, as Johan Huizinga suggests. With respect to ARGs it would be more productive to focus on how the players *apply a playful perspective to the everyday scene*. I argue that in ARGs and LBGs there is no clear separation between the game world and the ordinary world: instead the ordinary world is present during and within the game. In this discussion, the term 'integration' is introduced. Integration describes the process whereby the players integrate their surroundings into the game or a situation in which a person accepts an invitation to play when he/she is not playing. These games seem to be magically circling around the player, into and out of everyday life. This idea will be explored further throughout the chapter.

The concept of the magic circle will be presented here in order to show how two aspects of ARGs and LBGs contradict it. These aspects are the situations in which: 1) the players integrate the ordinary world into the game world, and 2) the game breaks through into the ordinary world.

My goal is to give a more accurate description of the relation between the player, the game world, and the ordinary world than is currently available. This description will draw on the theories of Johan Huizinga (1993), Michael Apter (1991), Bo Kampmann Walther (2007a), Jane McGonigal (2003), and Katie Salen and Eric Zimmerman (2004). I use examples from very different kinds of games only to state the fact that the new generation of games needs a new approach – an approach that allows designers to play with uncertainty and that challenges the players' ability to create meaning. The ideas presented here could also work as background information for the design of an LBG that employs positioning technology and uses the physical position of the player as an element in the game.

Huizinga's theory is the starting point for this chapter; let us begin by entering the idea of the magical circle and its implications.

1. THE MAGIC CIRCLE

Huizinga developed his theory on play as part of 1930s culture. This was an era long before the technology used for ARGs and LBGs was invented. However, Huizinga's theory is still discussed in game research, and has been related to both ARGs and LBGs. According to him, rules *separate* play from the ordinary world, and as soon as the players accept the rules, they enter a space with a special meaning (Huizinga 1993). Among other metaphors Huizinga uses the term 'magic circle' to describe this space, an area of activity that is temporary and has its own rules. For instance, when engaging in a soccer match the players know that there is a start and an end to the game that are both signalled by the whistle. The players also know that the rules of the game apply within the outlined physical area. For Huizinga, the game differs from ordinary life by its position in time and space: it happens within certain spatial and time limits and it carries its meaning and sequence in itself. This "isolation" and "limitation" from the ordinary world is characteristic of play according to Huizinga (1993).

Huizinga states that the rules of a game are fixed; they should be unambiguous and reliable so that the player has no doubt about them. If we return to the soccer game then this would mean that all players have to know that the rules are not up for discussion – though this is not the case when we consider the referee's interpretation of events according to the rules. Huizinga (1993) claims that every time the referee blows the whistle the magic circle will be broken, so that the players have to re-establish it afterwards by going back into play.

Play is fragile: at every moment ordinary life can interfere. An external disturbance can cause a breakdown. The circle will also break if a player breaks the rules of the game, or when players discuss these rules, or even because of the players' disappointment or disillusion (Huizinga 1993). Huizinga consequently emphasises that although it is crucial to the game that the players maintain the magic circle by following rules that are beyond doubt, it is also important that the game is interesting. Players are thus constantly shifting between being *in* play and *out* of play.

Huizinga (1993) claims that doubt about rules can spoil the experience of play and break the magic circle. But this begs the question: what exactly are "rules"? As Huizinga does not offer a precise definition of rules, I draw on the work of game theorists Katie Salen and Eric Zimmerman (2004), who relate Huizinga's theory to digital games. According to them, the rules of the game limit the possibilities available to the players, and the goal of the game makes it possible to judge which possibilities are relevant in order to reach that goal. In other words, what Huizinga is saying is that players should know the possibilities open to them, what is not allowed, and what is relevant to the game: they should know what actions are meaningful in the game.

When games are played on the boundary between play and ordinary life, can we make such a clear cut distinction between being in play and out of play? When a player is approaching a game challenge on the street, navigating traffic and passers-by, does the player then feel isolated and limited from the ordinary world? Play itself needs to be approached from a different angle to discuss this. The views of the American psychologist Michael Apter, presented in the following section, will inform this new approach.

2. MODES NOT CIRCLES

Huizinga presents one view of the players' relation to the game world and the ordinary world. The perspective of the magical circle, sees play as constituted by free actions which do not have a serious intention and are without a useful purpose. Rules limit these actions and separate the player from the ordinary world (Huizinga 1993). There is a difference between this view and the position presented by psychologist Michael Apter. Apter defines play as "a state of mind, a way of seeing and being, a special mental 'set' towards the world and ones actions in it" (Apter 1991, 13). This definition presents play as a perspective on the world that cannot be described fully as a certain kind of action.

According to Apter (1989), the concept of motivation is vital to any understanding of human actions. People's perception of their motivation consists of three elements according to Apter (1989). Motivation is a combination of

- A sense of the level of *arousal,*
- An idea of a *goal* that one has to strive for, and
- A sense of the possible *means* to an end.

Arousal is a measure of how 'worked up' a person is or how emotionally affected a person feels at a given time. The level of arousal is related to the "Hedonic tone", which describes how much or how little pleasure a person takes in a situation (Apter 1989).

Following a *goal* is seen by some as the primary driver for actions. However, according to Apter the goal is not an explanation of motivation in itse;f/ If the goal is the main motivation for an action then the person focusing on this goal will probably consider which activity will lead most effectively to its attainment. If the person does not succeed, then the activity would have been a waste of time and effort. But this does not apply to all activities; some activities are carried out because they are a source of joy in themselves (Apter 1989). These are activities that are playful, and whilst doing them the person's focus is on the process and the means rather than the ends. Certain types of activities do not necessarily determine this approach: a person can be playful and working, or goal-oriented and engaged in a game. Shifts between being oriented against the goal or the process can also occur within an activity.

To be motivated the player also needs to have relevant *means* to pursue the goal. In relation to games, means are relevant when they affect the player's arousal in a pleasurable way, and preferably help the player approach the goal. Meaningful actions are thus actions performed with an intention within the context of the game.

As an example, a player can be playful while playing a game: he tries out new combinations, feels excited about playing, and enjoys himself, and sometimes he fails, sometimes he wins. Then the player meets a challenge that is way above his skill level. Every time he tries to win, he is badly beaten and cannot seem to get any closer to ending the level. He gets frustrated and suddenly his goal is more important than the process of playing the game. This makes the difference between a playful and a non-playful approach.

Apter uses the term "paratelic" to define the process-oriented and playful approach and the term "telic" for the goal-oriented and serious approach (Apter 1989). These two terms are actually "meta-motivational" states which control a persons' desired state of arousal, i.e. it decides whether the person will experience pleasure at high arousal or low arousal. Motivation, on the other hand, is the function that regulates a person's mood. Through motivation, the person can achieve the desired level of arousal defined by the meta-motivation (Apter 1989). A person with a paratelic approach is in a meta-motivational state that gives him a need to feel high arousal and excitement, whereas a person in a telic state will strive for activities that lower their level of arousal. The meta-motivational state defines what the player will be motivated to do, and the rules of the game should offer limited possibilities that might be relevant in order to reach arousal (Apter 1991).

While playing a game the player can shift between having a playful approach to a more serious approach, and vice-versa (Apter 1991). However, a person cannot consciously control such shifts, according to Apter. What happens is that the strongest force in the moment decides what mode the individual is in; it is a sort of fight between influences. It is possible to control the shift indirectly, however, by offering the right circumstances for it to take place (Apter 1991).

A person in the paratelic mode is willing to experiment, to play around, to fantasise and to make believe (Apter, 1991). Apter does not talk of a magic circle, but he claims that in the paratelic state (in play) a psychological bubble encapsulates us, so that we feel secure and unthreatened (Apter 1991). According to Apter, when playing or gaming, we create a little controllable private world, which we can choose to share with others. Outside this world, nothing is meaningful, as long as we are in game. We are ultimately managing and controlling in the game/play world, and what we do is voluntary (Apter 1991). The protective frame that Apter describes exists between the player and the ordinary world and it is mainly psychological, but it can have physical representation or an abstract form – such as the rules in a game (Apter 1991). He states that if the "real world" does enter in some way, it causes no harm. Here is the difference between the two theories: Huizinga's magic circle will break if everyday life enters it, whereas Apter's bubble removes harm from everyday life but also allows it to enter (Apter 1991). Apter uses an analogy about a tiger in a cage to describe this. He states that a tiger without a cage produces anxiety in people; But a cage without the tiger causes boredom. Only a tiger in a cage produces excitement, because it is danger within safety (Apter 1991). McGonigal takes this idea a step further in relating it to the design of ARGs:

perhaps the central goal of successful immersive game design is to communicate to players that a cage is in place, while making it as easy and likely as possible for the players to pretend that they don't see the cage. In other words, I suggested, give the audience a tiger, build a sturdy and always visible cage, but give the crowd both the means and the incentive to say, "What cage? I don't see a cage" even as the spectators are "oohing" and "aahing" over the cage's lovely gilt design and breathtaking size. (McGonigal 2003)

The point here is that it is still possible to distinguish between the ordinary world and the game world; it is visible to the players but they try not to see it. This leads to the idea of integration: if the players are trying to ignore the limit between the ordinary world and the game world then it makes sense that they try to integrate the borderline situations into the game world. Players connect their experiences from the ordinary world with play (Copier 2005).

I am presenting this view because it is a different approach to the relation between the ordinary world, the game world, and the player. It is important to understand how everyday life can be a part of the game world and that objects from everyday life can be a part of game-play in relation to games played in the sphere of the ordinary. In the next section, I will look closer at what happens when players find themselves in such ambiguous situations and how they handle them.

3. PERVADING THE ORDINARY: CASES

When playing ARGs and LBGs players confront the everyday world with the question "Is this part of the game?" Both types of games are about experiencing gaming affordances of everyday spaces (McGonigal 2006; 2007). The ARGs also have a "this is not a game" rhetoric, which plays with the distinction between the game world and the ordinary world as the game tries to erase the boundary between the two to claim that it is not a game (McGonigal 2003).

An example is the ARG called Go Game, which is an "urban superhero game produced by Wink Back, Inc. that bills itself as a combination of Mission Impossible,[2] performance art and scavenger hunt" (McGonigal 2003,

---

2 An action movie about an CIA agent that tries to clean his name as he is framed for being the culprit of a failed mission where his wife died (http://imdb.com/title/tt0117060/plotsummary)

20). In Go Game, teams of four to eight persons cooperate to solve missions in order to beat other groups. The game missions are downloaded to each player's web-enabled cell phone and then they head out in the streets of a city, competing with one another. Planted clues, missions, and trivia are woven together by wireless technology. The answers to the challenges are given in the form of digital photographs, digital video, audio recordings, and text input.[3] An example of such a mission was to find a particular massive overpass with limited public access where the team must hang a banner with a three-word political message (McGonigal 2003). The team rushed into the lobby of a Hilton Hotel near a suitable overpass that they had found. The players had to look for someone who could help them get access to the overpass. As the game used "plants", i.e. actors who play a role in the game, then it was logical for them to think that when a friendly hotel worker approached them he was part of the game (McGonigal 2003). After much convincing, he finally helped them and they got the banner in place. After the game, they said this event was the most interesting. When they found out that the person was not even part of the game they were even more thrilled. McGonigal makes this conclusion in her article about this incident: "They had projected the game onto reality, and reality had conformed to their game expectations" (McGonigal 2003, 20). This example shows clearly how the ambiguity of a game's relationship with the real world is part of game play. Players have incorporated the framework of the game into their everyday lives, and experience their surroundings through this frame. They make a meaningful connection between the task and the ordinary environment that they are in: they project play onto their surroundings. It is part of the fun that the players do not know where the boundaries are between the game world and the ordinary world. Play and everyday life are not separated; players are not isolated from the ordinary world, though the game has a meaningfulness that distinguishes the hotel lobby in the game from the same environment out of the game. It acquires meaning through their actions – it is the player's attitude towards the lobby, their playful approach, that creates the boundary between play and non-play. Here the idea of the magic circle is proved wrong, but the situation does not contradict Apter's theory.

InGo Game, there is another example of how players apply the game world to the everyday world. A group of players sat down and "chanted

---

3   http://www.thegogame.com/team/game/description/intro.asp

mantras" as they were hoping for "spiritual guidance" from a person that they thought was part of the game – but he was not. Although they realised this after some time, they still concluded that the game tried to teach them to have patience. The event actually increased their experience of playing the game (McGonigal 2003). They simply created a story and a reason for the incident which made it meaningful to the game. This example demonstrates that the boundary between the game world and the ordinary world can be blurred, and that finding out what is relevant to the game is one of the challenges to the players. The example also shows that the players embrace events from the ordinary world and *give* them meaning within the game. Players are productive: they *integrate* non-game events into the game.

It is also possible to demonstrate how an ARG breaks into the ordinary world. What is this Game? is an ARG that uses Internet websites, movie clips, a forum, and e-mails as channels through which its players can find clues, discuss and analyse them, and contact fictional persons. The object of What is this Game? is to find six "contracts" that are well hidden and defended by "guardians". The first five contracts are common to all players, signifying the end of each stage, while the sixth and final contract is only granted to the winner.[4] When registered to play the game, you log in to the main game website on the Internet. Here the first mission is given: to find the host by finding a webpage. Clues are found in the welcome text, and players discuss them on a game forum. When the webpage is found the next clue is given and the players are sent further out into the Internet. This game is still ongoing.

In my experience of the game, I was contacted in person by email. This email aroused my curiosity, interrupting my serious state of mind with a shift to a more playful state. The game caused a change in my motivation. According to Apter (1989), people always seek pleasure. Sometimes a person will feel pleasure at high arousal, sometimes at low arousal; motivation regulates the choice of activities to help reach the level that will give pleasure at that specific time (Apter 1989). Sometimes a person will feel pleasure in pursuing and making progress towards a goal; at other times they will derive pleasure from the activity itself (Apter 1989). In ARGs like What is this game?, the player can be contacted at any time and in any mood. They might be in a playful mood, but it is just as likely that they are in a serious state of mind and not seeking play. The person will shift from a telic state to

---

4   http://whatisthisgame.wikidot.com/

a paratelic sonly if it is meaningful for them, as the game is not forced upon him. In this case, a meaningful action is one that would raise the player's arousal as they would be in a paratelic state.

Players in a playful state of mind can amplify their game experience. I observed this at the Open Air Museum in Brede, Denmark, where two boys were playing the LBG Land of Possibilities?, a game about immigration from Denmark to the US at the end of the 19th century. The boys were looking for the home of their avatar "Jens." It was quite a challenge for them to find the farm. They had a hand drawn map of the area with which to navigate, but their GPS did not have a satellite connection, which meant that they could not see their own location on the map, and the map itself was not updating. At one point, they found a house that could have been the right one, but nothing happened on their device. They double-checked the map, then tried to open the doors of the farm, but they were locked and so they called out if Jens was there. One of the boys said: "Maybe we should knock first."[5] He then knocked on the door of the farm, perhaps expecting some-one to answer, but no one did. By actually knocking on the door, the player extends the LBG into physical space, acting out the logic of the game. This house could have become a *place* in the two boys' game experience, provided that they found it meaningful. They searched for the house, interacted with it, and invested it with added meaning: they have drawn it into their play space.

Players of the LBG Foursquare also create places as a part of the game when they set up venues. Players use their smart phones to set up a venue, a location that appears on a map for other players to find and "check in to". Creating a venue tells other players that the location has significance, but also displays the player's own intention. As an example, one Foursquare player has created a location called "Platform 9 ¾" at Kings Cross Station in London. This is a reference to the *Harry Potter* story universe (Rowling 1997), in which young wizards use this platform to travel to their school, Hogwarts; to gain access to the platform, the wizards must run into a wall, which they can magically pass through. *Foursquare* players have checked into the venue and left the following comments: "You have to run at it hard! No hesitation!"; "If it's good enough for Harry Potter, it's good enough for me"; "Just be sure not to run into the wrong wall"; "Careful U might run to a real wall"; and "I came here last week. The steps are as follows: 1: Run at

---

5   This is expressed in Danish: "Det kunne være, vi skulle banke på først."

the platform as fast as you can. 2: Enjoy Hogwarts until you wake up from your head injury" (Foursquare 2010). Obviously, the players are creating the significance of this place together, turning it into a collectively understood platform for interaction (Gordon 2009). They are inviting others to play and these invitations are distributed into space as latent offers waiting to be found. The players are looking for and offering ways into meaningful play.

When Huizinga (1993) characterises play, he states that it has a definite beginning, end, and sequence. There is a limit between play and the ordinary world that is established by its rules, which isolates the player from the ordinary world. However, this does not seem to be the case for these games. What Is This Game? is circling magically around the player, *contacting* them by email and offering play from time to time. Foursquare lies around in public spaces leaving invitations for players to pick up when it suits them. Foursquare can even contact players when friends are close by. These examples are also important because the players actually set the limits of the games themselves, integrating places and people into the play. This differentiates ARGs and LBGs from digital games that have engineered experience settings.

Huizinga (1993) claims that play has a meaningful function. In the examples described above, sense making does play an important role, as the players integrate "off-game" elements into the game by giving them sense in the game. It could therefore be said that the players use the possibilities available to them and they choose those that can help them achieve their goal in the game; as their levels of arousal are increased in this way, their actions are meaningful. In the cases above it seems as though players choose possibilities that increase arousal and that they hope will help them to reach their "in-game" goal.

4. INTEGRATING RELEVANT OBJECTS INTO THE GAME-WORLD

When we look at games set in the ordinary world, we must challenge Huizinga's recognised theory in order to appreciate an appealing game in which the idea of pervading ordinary space makes (greater) sense than thinking about isolation and separation. As we have seen in the examples give above, players take some events from the ordinary world into play, giving them meaning in the game.

In ARGs and LBGs *everyday life* or *the ordinary world* is used as an extension of the game world. Here objects can have an ambiguous meaning:

objects in the ordinary world can also simultaneously be objects that make sense within the game world (Walther 2007a). In order to make sense in the game world, the objects have to be integrated into the game and thus tied to an action and ultimately to the goal of the game – if we follow Salen and Zimmerman's definition of rules. However, it seems like players themselves give sense to the situations they meet and thereby set the limits of the circle by playing, both because they want to believe in the game world and because they are excited by the idea that they can apply the game to the everyday world (Nieuwdorp 2007).

In this way, the game "blurs the boundaries between itself and the ordinary world which can influence the concept of the magic circle" (Nieuwdorp 2007, 3). This does not mean that the players cannot distinguish between the everyday world and the game world (McGonigal, 2003), but when they play, it is not always clear if the situation or object that they are approaching is part of either world. The players use the rules, story, and the goal of the game to establish the boundary – integrating what can be interpreted as relevant (but is not necessarily actually relevant) to the game, as seen in the examples above. The actions of the players in the examples still have relevance because they add to the players' experience and pleasure, in accordance with Apter's theory.

What does this change in understanding of play actually mean when we approach games set in ordinary space? It means that the designers of ARGs and LBGs have to think about integration instead of separation: the designer should leave room for doubt about the scope of the game and should not hesitate to give an already known object new meaning in the game, leaving room for its interpretation. Using ambiguity in an LBG places a greater demand on the player to create meaning, and potentially results in a more exciting play experience (Gaver, Beaver, & Benford 2003). This integration is explored in the design of the LBG (Ejsing-Duun 2011). *Visions of Sara* has been created to explore the possibilities of the LBG's spatial aspects. It is also part of a practice, and has been running for over two years at the central library in Odense, Odense Centralbibliotek. The game is a site-specific LBG in which multiple players cooperate in groups that compete against other groups. The storyline is takes place in both the 16th century and the present day, and involves ghosts, mysteries, riddles, and a murder. Through the design of this game, paths have been engineered to promote the sensuous involvement of players, locations have been framed as part of the narrative, and a framework has been developed that allows players to incorporate elements into the game themselves.

5. CONCLUSION

Instead of separating the player from the ordinary world, I have argued that the ordinary world is still present within the game, although its meaning can be different depending on the player's sense-making approach. The ordinary world cannot threaten the player and together with the player's motivation the rules and goals of the game delineate a framework used for giving meaning to objects as part of the game – if they are not explicitly excluded. I argue that players have an ability to make 'gaming sense' and to approach the ordinary world with a playful mindset when playing games set in ordinary space – like LBGs and ARGs.

I have explored this topic even further by designing the LBG *Visions of Sara*, set in Odense, Denmark, and analysing four more LBGs (Ejsing-Duun 2011). Through this study I have observed how players come into play situations with experiences from other games, using technology and knowledge that they draw on when they play. They use the game as a tool to use this prior knowledge. They thus adjust to the rules and goal of the game; in this way, the game directs the player's action and attention. In other words, in the play situation the intentionality of both the player and the game exist simultaneously. Players learn the dynamics of the game through play, attending to the feedback and the consequences of their actions. This structures the player's attention and actions during play in ordinary space (Ejsing-Duun 2011). Players create connections between play and ordinary life, drawing on their knowledge from everyday life, acting out the game in the streets, and approaching the everyday environment in a playful state of mind, ready to find the gaming possibilities in the ordinary. LBGs and ARGs provide players with a framework which they can use to distinguish between which elements of the ordinary are relevant in play and which are not. It is the players that make the magic happen, using the game as a tool.

REFERENCES

Apter, M. 1989. *Reversal Theory – Motivation, Emotion and Personality*. London: Routledge.

Apter, M. 1991."A structural-phenomenology of play." In *Adult Play: A Reversal Theory Approach*, edited by J. H. K. M. J. Apter, 13-25. Amsterdam/Lisse: Swets & Zeitlinger.

Copier, M. 2005. "Connecting Worlds. Fantasy Role-Playing Games, Ritual Acts and the Magic Circle." Paper presented at the Changing Views: Worlds in Play:

Proceedings of the 2005 Digital Games Research Association Conference, Vancouver, June.

Ejsing-Duun, S. 2011, In Press. *Location-Based Games: From Street to Screen.* Copenhagen: Aarhus University Press.

Foursquare. 2010. "Foursquare: Platform 9 3/4." Available at http://foursquare.com/venue/347147, accessed on October 30, 2010.

Gaver, W. W., J. Beaver, & S. Benford. 2003. "Ambiguity as a resource for design." In *Proceedings of the SIGCHI conference on Human factors in computing systems.* Ft. Lauderdale, Florida, USA: ACM.

Gordon, E. 2009. "Redefining the Local. The Distinction between Located Information and Local Knowledge in Location-Based Games." In *Digital cityscapes – merging digital and urban playspaces*, edited by A. de Souza e Silva & D. Sutko, 21-36. New York: Peter Lang.

Huizinga, J. 1993. *Homo Ludens: Om kulturen oprindelse i leg (Eng.: Homo Ludens. A study of the play element in culture)*, 2nd ed., translated by N. C. Lindtner. Copenhagen: Gyldendal.

McGonigal, J. 2003. "A Real Little Game: The Performance of Belief in Pervasive Play." In *Digital Games Research Associaton (DiGRA) "Level Up" Conference Proceedings*. University of Utrecht, The Netherlands.

McGonigal, J. 2006. "This Might Be a Game: Ubiquitous Play and Performance at the Turn of the Twenty-First Century." PhD Diss., University of California, Berkeley.

McGonigal, J. 2007. "Ubiquitous Gaming. A Vision for the Future of Enchanted Spaces." In *Space, Time, Play. Computer Games, Architecture and Urbanism: The Next Level*, edited byF. v. Borries, S. P. Walz, & M. Böttger, 233-237. Basel, Boston, Berlin: Birkhäuser.

Nieuwdorp, E. 2007. "The Pervasive Discourse: An Analysis." *ACM Computers in Entertainment*, Vol. 5 (2, Article 13).

Rowling, J. K. 1997. *Harry Potter and the Philosopher's Stone.* London: Bloomsbury.

Salen, K. & E. Zimmerman. 2004. *Rules of Play. Game Design Fundamentals.* The MIT Press.

Walther, B. K. 2007a. "Pervasive Game-Play: Theoretical Reflection and Classifications." In *Concepts and Technologies for Pervasive Games – A Reader for Pervasive Gaming Research*, vol. 1, edited by C. Magerkurth & C. Röcker, 67-90. Leipzig: Shaker Verlag.

6. GAME-BASED LEARNING'S STRUGGLE FOR ADAPTATION

INTERNATIONAL SURVEY ON THE EXPERIENCES AND PERCEPTIONS OF TEACHERS

Simon Egenfeldt-Nielsen

1. INTRODUCTION

This paper presents the results from an online survey undertaken in Denmark, Finland, Norway, Portugal, and the United States with 275 respondents. The majority of respondents were Danish teachers and they will therefore serve as a reference point for the analysis and discussions.

The survey finds that the use of computer games in the educational system is widespread, with around 60 % of all teachers having used games. This was the case across all participating countries, and there was particularly high adaptation among female teachers in the lower grades.

In general, teachers recognise the potential of computer games especially for skills and topics education but perceive barriers to ICTs as numerous, the most frequently mentioned ones being practical barriers like computer equipment and installation. Teachers feel that students achieve good learning outcomes from games, and that boys and disadvantaged students benefit from them in particular. Usually teachers learn about using games from other teachers and prefer to go to them for help in selecting which computer games to use in their lessons.

2. THE SURVEY

As we saw in the introductory chapter to this book the idea of using game-based learning is not new. It is possible to track and interest in the area over the last forty years, and perhaps longer, though the strength of and challenges to this interest have varied (Abt 1970, Loftus & Loftus 1983, Egenfeldt-Nielsen 2007). The situation today seems promising: game-based learning is the subject of many active research projects, conferences, media coverage, and initiatives withing education. Many positive research overviews in the broad area of learning from video games have appeared within the past twenty years (i.e. Cavallari et al. 1992, Dempsey et al. 1996, McGrenere 1996, Squire

2002, Kirriemuir & McFarlane 2003, Mitchell & Savill-Smith 2004, de Freitas 2007, Egenfeldt-Nielsen & Felicia 2011).

With all these facts at hand, we are justified in asking why game-based learning is not generally an integrated part of formal education. Game-based learning continues to be an unusual and only occasionally employed strategy for many teachers, which is apparent from studies conducted by FutureLab, the European Network of Schools, and also the survey presented in the current paper. Though many teachers use game-based learning, it does not seem to be a mainstream activity.

The current survey set out to examine the use of computer games in more detail than has been common in previous surveys on the topic; another key aim was to include countries that had not been addressed by previous studies. Previous studies have involved teachers from Spain, the United Kingdom, Italy, Denmark, Austria, France, Lithuania, and the Netherlands (Wastiau, Kearney, & Van den Berghe 2009). In the current study Denmark, Norway, Finland, Portugal, and the US were covered. The only country that overlaps with these previous studies is Denmark.

In some ways the results from the study described in this chapter are encouraging; a key finding was that teachers are interested in using games, but they see many barriers to putting this into practice.

3. PARTICIPANTS

The survey aimed to get an understanding of teachers' perceptions, current uses, and possible future uses of computer games in education. The survey had 275 respondents: from Denmark (185), Finland (34), United States (25), Norway (21), and Portugal (9). 66 % of the respondents were female. The age of the teachers was fairly representative, with a few more than one third of the total in each of the groups of 31-40 years, 41-50 years, and 51-60 years. The rest were evenly split between categories of teachers below 30 years and above 60 years old.

The participants' experience with ICT was normally distributed; experience with playing computer games approached normal distribution but skewed towards little experience. The teachers were representative with regard to the subjects they taught, the years of teaching experience they had, and the grades they taught.

4. METHOD

The survey was designed by a research group with extensive experience within the area, and based on previous surveys administered in the area by FutureLab (Williamson 2009) and the European School Network (Wastiau, Kearney, & Van den Berghe 2009). In total the survey consisted of 24-42 questions, the number depending on which branches the respondent selected. The first 6 questions related to general background, including subjects like gender, age, and previous general experience. Then the survey branched into two sections, one for teachers who used games and one for those who did not. The teachers who used games answered 18 questions about duration, barriers, perception, type, outcome, inspiration, and other similar issues. At the end of this core survey, these teachers were asked to share concrete example of games they had used, and rate these in relation to 4 questions. They could repeat this question three times. In contrast teachers that did not use games only received 4 questions about why games were not a part of their teaching. The survey consisted mainly of closed questions with two open questions in the last two categories.

The survey was administered by e-mail through identical but translated surveys to fit the local terminology for school curricula and subjects. Initially we selected representative primary schools and lower secondary schools in Denmark, Norway, Finland, the United States, and Portugal. The goal was to prioritise the collection of responses from these schools to ensure that we received a fair selection of teachers from a given school instead of just a few teachers from different places who were particularly interested in games. The schools were informed that the teacher who participated in the survey would be entered in a draw for a prize.

Initially, an email requesting participation was sent to the principal of each school, who was then contacted by phone at least three times to increase the chances of the survey being administered to teachers. If the principal was unreachable, the school secretary was approached by phone. Finally, in Denmark posters were distributed to be put up in staff rooms, with the help of the school secretary.

Unfortunately, the response rate from teachers was still very low in terms of the total number of teachers, which questions how representative the sample is. We did talk to researchers who had conducted similar studies, and they had simply distributed their survey through their mailing list. In this sense we believe that our approach was more balanced, as our respondents were not selected from forums that were aimed at teachers interested in games. However, the risk of self-selection is still present.

We did ask for a number of items of background data to ensure that our respondents were a representative sample of the teacher population. In this regard, the respondents do look representative across aspects of teaching experience, subjects covered, grade level taught, ICT experience, game experience, and gender selection.

The results were analysed using SPSS 16; basic descriptive statistics and cross-tabulations were employed to test whether key findings were statistically significant at 0,05.

5. RESULTS

The results of the study are presented below. Most tables present the results in the following categories: all respondents, female/male respondents, and DK/World teachers. "DK" signifies Danish teachers; teachers from the remaining countries are represented by the "World" figures. The statistics are not split into individual countries as some of them had quite small samples.

5.1. GETTING STARTED AND CHOOSING A GAME

The survey indicates that it is difficult to penetrate the market with a new game. In general, teachers have stated that they start teaching with games based on their own interest (36 %) or on recommendations from other teachers (25 %). Danish teachers have a higher tendency than Western teachers worldwide to start using a game after a training course or seeing coverage of the game in a professional magazine. 30 % of the Danish teachers started using a game after a course or seeing coverage, with 15 % learning about the game from each method. This is compared to only 9 % in total for Western teachers worldwide. On the other hand, teachers outside Denmark are considerably more likely to have started using games after receiving marketing material. In countries outside Denmark 18 % of the teachers who used games started after receiving marketing material, whereas in Denmark that figure is only 6 %.

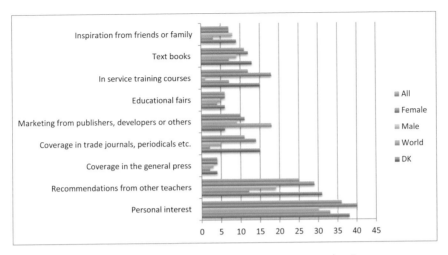

Table 1: *How did you first get started using computer games in your teaching?*

The tendency of a more closed circuit approach with regard to teachers' inspiration for using games in Denmark is also confirmed when we asked teachers more directly about how they actually choose a game. Here personal judgment (42 %) and recommendation from other teachers (33 %) also scored highly. After that follows coverage in trade journals (16 %), textbooks (12 %), and marketing from publishers (11 %). The most noticeable difference is that Danish teachers are more receptive to trade journals than Western teachers worldwide. 20 % of Danish teachers mentioned these, compared to only 8 % of Western teachers worldwide. On the other hand, Western teachers are more susceptible to marketing with 16 % mentioning this compared to only 9 % in Denmark.

5.2. ADAPTATION

The survey finds that 60 % of all teachers use computer games in their teaching. The Danish adaptation is higher with around 62.7 % of all teachers using games, whereas worldwide it is only 51.7 %. This is in contrast to the resultsof the study by the European School Network, which found that 70.6 % use games. However, this may be explained by the higher self-selection bias in the survey, because although the recruitment was done through neutral newsletters there was not an incentive for teachers that did not have a specific reason for participating, as there was in our study. When you subtract Lithuania (37 %) from their numbers it becomes even higher. On the other hand, the United Kingdom is somewhat above their average with a figure of 85 % suggesting that they are still the leading country in Europe for adapting to game-based learning. For Denmark, which is the only comparable country, they found 77 % compared to the 62.7 % in our study. As the Danish sample size in our study is 185, against the 28 respondents in the study conducted by the European School Network, the current survey should be more precise.

In the current study there is an indication that female teachers use computer games more than male teachers. Overall 63.5 % of female teachers had used games, whereas for male teachers that figure is only 51.1 %. However, looking more closely at these numbers it becomes clear that female teachers are only more likely to be users of game-based learning if they teach in the lower grades. Female teachers use games significantly more in grades 1-3, but not in other grades.

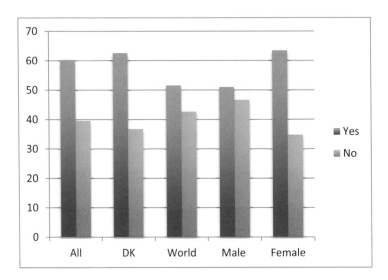

Table 2: *How many teachers have used computer games in teaching?*

It is also clear that the adaption to using computer games in education is in general higher in the lower grades, which also fits well with the use patterns in regard to what type of games are used and for what learning purpose. When we look at the purposes of the games which teachers used, two stand out: games designed to teach learning skills (52 %) and specific topics (23 %). The rest of the teachers were split pretty evenly between finding games useful in teaching about them as a medium, in enhancing pupils' creative/production skills, in inter-disciplinary teaching, or simply for entertainment.

SERIOUS GAMES IN EDUCATION

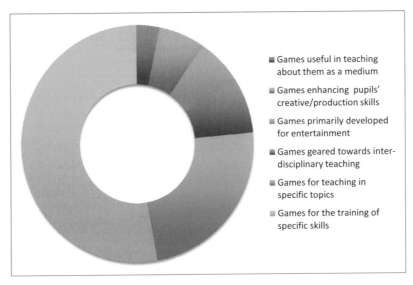

Table 3: *What type of games have you used in your teaching?*

Almost 90 % of all teachers tend to use games in fewer than three lessons at a time, but the Danish teachers tended to favour a longer duration over Western teachers worldwide. In Denmark only 42 % of the teachers used games for the duration of 0-1 lessons, whereas the percentage of Western teachers worldwide in this category is 70 %. Also, considerably more Danish teachers suggest that the optimal duration of a course involving a game is more than 3 lessons.

5.3. ATTITUDES AND REASONS

The aim of this study was not only to examine whether teachers used games, but for what reasons and how they valued them. It became clear in the survey that few teachers dismissed games outright, but also that only a few valued them for their learning capabilities. The teachers generally had a "wait and see" attitude towards games.

The majority of teachers took a cautious approach to computer games, describing their attitudes as experimental, or stating that the use of games requires careful control. On the other hand, the idea of computer games as a motivational tool did not gather much support – only around 12 %, regardless of gender and territory, stressed this. So it is quite interesting that the two main focus areas of academic studies in game-based learning carried relatively little weight, which suggests that this is indeed still very much an experimental praxis.

The legend of the figure reads:

- Games useful in teaching about them as a medium
- Games enhancing pupils' creative/production skills
- Games primarily developed for entertainment
- Games geared towards inter-disciplinary teaching
- Games for teaching in specific topics
- Games for the training of specific skills

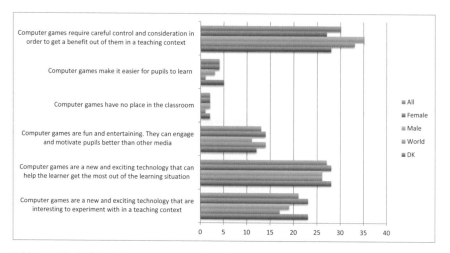

Table 4: *Which of the following statements best describes your attitude towards the use of computer games in classes?*

When we look more directly at the rationale for using computer games it becomes clear that quite a few teachers are in doubt of the merits of games, as many simply point to variety (40 %), but engagement (40 %) and differentiation (28 %) also scored highly. This fragmentation is also in line with the results from the European School Network, in which the three highest-scoring reasons for using games were: an increase in pupils' motivation (27 %); a contribution to educational goals (24 %); and the ability to use them in a flexible way (21 %) (Wastiau, Kearney, & Van den Berghe 2009). The strong support for engagement as a rationale for using games seems to be in opposition to the fact that only 12 % of teachers perceive games primarily as a teaching strategy that can engage and motivate. However, the explanation for these seemingly contradictory findings may be that many teachers find engagement/motivation an important part of games, but it is not their dominant perception of them.

There are some noticeable regional differences. Danish teachers, for example, seem to appreciate more rationales for using games. In Denmark around 50 % of the teachers state that variety, engagement, and differentiation are their main reasons for using games. The first two scored a little higher in Denmark – among Western teachers worldwide these reasons only scored 40 % – but differentiation is a much more important rationale for Danish teachers, as only 28 % of worldwide teachers mention this reason. However, the most noticeable difference between the two categories is in using games to get more out of learning. In Denmark 27 % of teachers gave this as a reason to use games in teaching, compared to only 7 % of worldwide teachers.

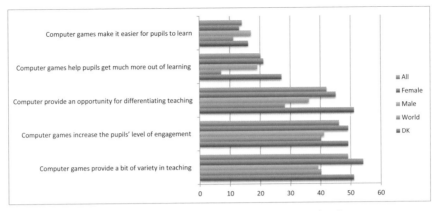

Table 5: *What are your reasons for using computer games in your teaching?*

5.4. BARRIERS

The problem of identifying barriers to game-based learning has received a lot of attention in previous research, and the findings are in line with the studies conducted by FutureLab (Williamson 2009) and European School Network (Wastiau, Kearney, & Van den Berghe 2009). The European School Network study is especially relevant here, as it also focuses on the educational use of games in general. Their survey did not ask about the same barriers, and have fewer questions related to the actual practical barriers; however, the practical barriers they did include in their fixed list were considered important by the teachers they asked. In their fixed questions, the European School Network found that the cost and licensing of games, the timetable of the school, and finding suitable games for teaching were identified as the biggest barriers by most teachers. However, the open questions gave a different picture: here it became apparent that hardware and installation are major issues. This finding is also supported by our study; in other words, nothing seems to have changed with regards to this issue in the two years between the studies.

The overall findings of this study are slightly discouraging if one wishes to talk about the wider adaptation of education systems to game-based learning, primarily because the most significant barriers to this adaptation are not really games-related, but rather due to the limitations of the ICT infrastructure. When we collate the findings about practical barriers, we can see that 58 % of all teachers identify practical barriers as among the top three barriers. So problems relating to computer equipment, installing the software, and the physical environment comes before any consideration of actually teaching with games.

Beyond the practical problems that are basically the result of an immature ICT infrastructure and setting in the educational system, we find more classic challenges to the use of games in teaching. These are that computer games are too expensive (18 %), learning games are not on par with other games (15 %), and individual teacher lack knowledge about teaching with games (10 %). Although many teachers appreciate that there are other barriers, these are dwarfed in significance by practical issues when teachers are asked to prioritise them.

From a global perspective, it looks like Denmark is slipping behind in terms of ICT, as more Danish teachers are worrying about the practical barriers to using computer games in their classes. 38 % of the Danish teachers asked saw problems with computer equipment as a barrier, compared to only 27 % of the Western teachers worldwide.

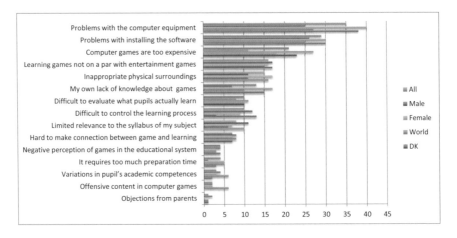

Table 6: *What are the barriers to using computer games in your teaching?*

5.5. LEARNING OUTCOMES

Overall, teachers are positive towards the learning outcomes it is possible to achieve by using computer games; although the majority do not see any major difference in teaching with games (78 %), 18 % believe that students will learn more from game-based teaching. This agrees with other findings that suggest that teachers do not use games specifically because of their learning potential, but rather for their usefulness as tools for variation, engagement, and differentiation (Wastiau, Kearney, & Van den Berghe 2009). Of course, it is still interesting that teachers do perceive games to be at least comparable to other teaching methods with regard to learning outcomes,

SERIOUS GAMES IN EDUCATION

and some even consider games to be better than other methods. It is also very interesting to look at the perceptions of the usefulness of games for teaching both 'weak' pupils and male pupils. 49 % of teachers believe that male pupils learn more from games. For weak pupils the findings are even clearer: 63 % of teachers find that these pupils learn more from games. The term 'weak' does not have a clear definition in the survey, but in general it is used to describe pupils who are perceived to experience different challenges that prevent them from achieving the expected academic level of the class. A negligible 3-4 % of teachers thought that weak pupils and male pupils may learn less from a teaching method involving games.

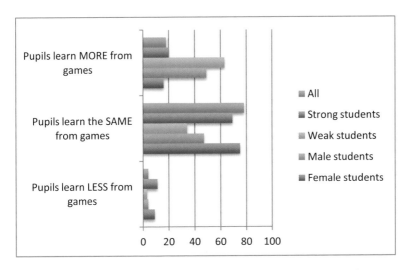

Table 7: *How would you characterise the pupils' learning outcome from a teaching session with games?*

Female and male teachers differ slightly in their opinions of the effect of games on overall learning outcomes; male teachers are more positive, stating that they think 26 % of students learn more from games, whilst female teachers think that this figure is only 15 %. Interestingly they do not differ in their perceptions of the effect of games on learning outcomes for boys: both believed that 50 % of boys will benefit. However, when it comes to female students they completely disagree. The male teachers thought that 26.2 % learn more from games, whereas that figure for female teachers is only 12.3 %. The male and female teachers are in agreement about the benefit for weak students, for whom more than 60 % of teachers think that games will help them learn more. However, for stronger students they disagree again. The male teachers were particularly polarised here; 26.2 % thought that strong students will learn more, but 16.7 % said they will learn less. Female teachers believed 17 % will learn more but only 9.4 % will learn less.

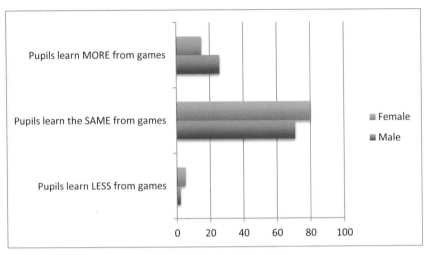

Table 8: *How do female and male teachers characterise the pupils' learning outcome from teaching with games?*

5.6. SUBJECT DIFFERENCES

To get a better feel for the differences between school subjects the survey results were analysed in relation to three major subjects: 'main subject',[6] maths, and foreign languages. The findings show that there are some differences between the use of games in teaching these subjects.

Maths is the subject in which games are used the most, with 70 % of teachers using them, followed by 57 % in the main subject, and then 52 % of foreign language teachers. This stands in some contrast to the fact that foreign language teaching has received some of the biggest investments during the last few years, but it is also notable that foreign language teachers believe that there is a larger potential for pupils to learn more from games in their subject, compared to teachers of other subjects. However, the differences across subjects are not that great, varying between 16 and 21 %.

---

6 'Main subject' is a broad term referring to the key subject in each country. In Denmark this is Danish, but other countries have different subject structures. The main subject usually centres around the mother language, but may also have other, broader learning goals

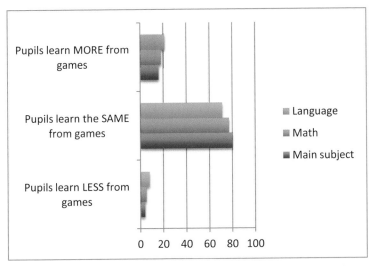

Table 9: *How would you characterise the pupils' learning outcome from a teaching session with games?*

A question that is often heard in the public debate about teaching with games is that older teachers may be more sceptical about this new method. This survey does supports this idea, but the picture is mixed. 33.3 % of teachers who have less than 5 years of experience thought that students learn more from computer games, whereas the figure for teachers with more than 26 years of experience is just 8.6 %. However, the two remaining groups did not answer the question in a way that was consistent with these results. Among the teachers with 6-15 years' experience, 14.9 % believed students learn more, but for those with 16-25 years' experience, 28 % agreed with this statement.

Looking at whether teachers actually use games or not makes the picture even more complicated. The teachers who use games the most are those with 6-15 years of experience. So there is not a natural fit between whether teachers believe games can provide better learning outcomes and whether they actually use them.

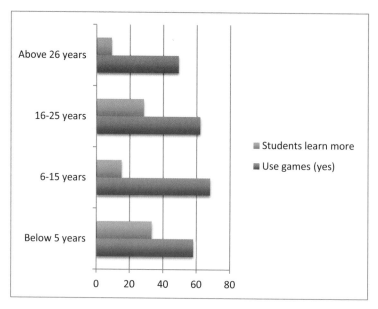

Table 10: *Shows how teachers evaluate the learning outcome of games and whether they use games in their teaching, according to how many years of experience they have in teaching.*

5.7. WHY GAMES SHOULD NOT BE USED

The major challenges for the teachers who have still not used games in their lessons are quite different from the challenges for those who actually have some experience with using games. We saw earlier that practical barriers account for a lot of the hesitation towards using games, but these are less of a concern for teachers who have not started using games yet. Though the practical barriers still exist, for these teachers the challenges to their use of games is much more about the changing learning process. Teachers identify the following problems: they have a lack of knowledge (40 %), they struggle to see the relevance to the syllabus (22 %), they find it hard to connect games and learning (20 %), and they consider it difficult to evaluate what pupils learn through games (15 %). Each of the practical barriers (computer equipment, installation, and settings) was identified by 20 % of the teachers, but it is interesting that this figure is lower than that derived from the answers of teachers who were already experienced with using games. This is a worry because it suggests that the perception of practical barriers is not alleviated when teachers begin to use games, but instead increases. To put it another way: practical issues are not a theoretical threat, but rather a real problem that grows as a teacher acquires more experience and sees the actual limitations of this teaching method.

SERIOUS GAMES IN EDUCATION

There are also some interesting gender differences, as more female teachers than male teachers believe they lack the necessary knowledge for teaching with games, find the games more expensive, and worry about the computer equipment. On the other hand, three times as many male teachers worry about the quality of the games used for teaching.

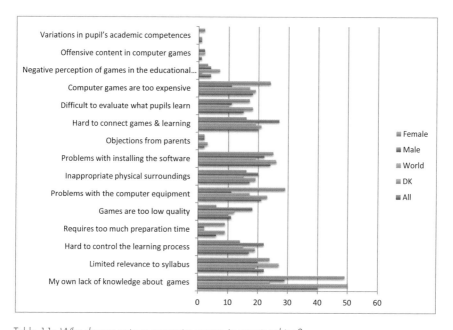

Table 11: *Why do you not use computer games in your teaching?*

6. CONCLUSION

In general, the results of this study are in accordance with previous studies conducted by FutureLab and the European School Network (Williamson 2009, Wastiau, Kearney, & Van den Berghe 2009). Our results show that there are limited differences across countries in terms of the use of games for teaching, although there are some outliers that were nevertheless less significant in the current study than the one conducted by the European School Network.

The adaptation to use games in teaching is quite high when one initially looks at the survey results. But further analysis of the results shows that most usage of games as a teaching method is concentrated in the lower grades, with female teachers leading the effort. It also becomes clear that most teachers still perceive games as an experimental teaching method that still has to prove itself. We have found that the reasons for using games are fragmented, but the barriers to using them are clear to most teachers. The practical barriers that prevent teachers starting to use games are very much part of the lack of adaptation.

Nevertheless, there is evidence that the majority of teachers see the learning potential of games, as they point to games as providing similar or better learning outcomes for students. This is especially true when we look at some of the groups that struggle in current educational system; it is suggested that weak students in particular will benefit from games, but this is also the case for male students. Male students may not always thrive in more traditional academic environments, so it makes sense that many teachers see male students benefiting from a different teaching method.

Despite the fact that computer games may have a huge potential for learning, it is unlikely that they will get a chance to prove themselves within the next few years as the infrastructure to do this is simply not in place. It is discouraging to see that despite years of investment in infrastructure and ICT skills for teaching, basic hardware and its installation are still considered the major barriers to using computer games in classes. Furthermore, it is important to stress that the prevalence of games does not seem to be directly related to teachers' experience. The teachers with less than 5 years of teaching experience actually use games less than their colleagues who have 6-25 years of experience, but more than the teachers with 26 or more years of experience. This shows that we cannot expect that games will automatically prevail as younger teachers take over; teachers probably need to have some experience of more traditional teaching methods before they start to use games, as the obstacles to game-based teaching are today very real.

It is our hope that the missing ICT infrastructure in schools does not perpetuate the current situation as regards game-based learning. Policy makers and school authorities need to recognise the importance of infrastructure if they want to harness the potential of new learning tools like computer games for future generations of students.

REFERENCES

de Freitas, S. 2007. *Learning in Immersive Worlds*. Joint Information Systems Committee. JISC Report. http://www.jisc.ac.uk/eli_outcomes.html accessed on November 1st 2011.

Egenfeldt-Nielsen, Simon S. (2007). *The Educational Potential of Computer Games*. New York: Continuum Press.

Egenfeldt-Nielsen, S. & P. Felicia. 2011. "Game-Based learning: a review of the state of the art." In (In press). Serious Games in Education – from a global perspective, edited by S. Egenfeldt-Nielsen, B. Meyer, & B. H. Sørensen. Aarhus: Aarhus University Press.

FutureLab. 2009. *NFER Teacher Voice Omnibus February 2009 Survey. Using computer games in the classroom*. Bristol: Futurelab.

McFarlane, A., A. Sparrowhawk, & Y. Heald. 2002. *Report on the educational use of games*. Teachers Evaluating Educational Multimedia. Cambridge.

Randel, J. M., B. A. Morris, C. D. Wetzel, & B. V. Whitehill. 1992. "The Effectiveness of Games for Educational Purposes: A Review of Recent Research." *Simulation & Gaming* 23(3): 261-276.

Sandford, R., M. Ulicsak, K. Facer, & T. Rudd. *Teaching with Games Using commercial off-the-shelf computer games in formal education*. Bristol: Futurelab.

Wastiau, P., C. Kearney, & W. Van den Berghe. 2009. *How are digital games used in schools? Final report*. Bruxelles: European School Network.

Williamson, B. 2009. *Computer games, schools, and young people: A report for educators on using games for learning*. Bristol: Futurelab. Available at www.futurelab.org.uk/resources/documents/project_reports/becta/Games_and_Learning_educators_report.pdf.